Contents

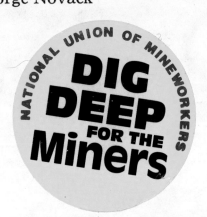

THE MARXIST THEORY OF ALIENATION

Three Essays by
ERNEST MANDEL
and
GEORGE NOVACK

WITHDRAWN

PATHFINDER PRESS

NEW YORK

The selection "Progressive Disalienation through the Building of Socialist Society, or the Inevitable Alienation in Industrial Society?" is reprinted from Ernest Mandel's *The Formation of the Economic Thought of Karl Marx*, translated by Brian Pearce, copyright © 1971 by Monthly Review Press and reprinted with permission of Monthly Review Press and New Left Books.

"The Causes of Alienation" by Ernest Mandel first appeared in the May 1970 issue of the *International Socialist Review* under the title "The Marxist Theory of Alienation."

"The Problem of Alienation" is a slightly revised version of an article that appeared first in the Fall 1959 issue of the *International Socialist Review*.

Library of Congress Card Catalog No. 72-96599

Pathfinder Press
410 West Street
New York, N.Y. 10014

Manufactured in the United States of America

COVER NOTE: Detail of a fresco by Diego Rivera. This panel, part of Rivera's "Portrait of America" series, was inspired by an actual punch press which was operated by manacled workers whose hands were automatically pulled back by the handcuffs each time the press descended. The advertising literature which provided Rivera's "model" boasted that the machine would yield "12,000 punches in a 9-hour day — as many punches per hour in the last hour as in the first."

Introduction

The problem of alienation as a condition of modern man has nowadays become an almost obsessive concern in areas of cultural activity ranging from literature and the plastic arts to sociology and philosophy. The isolated individual, like the central figure in *The Stranger* by Albert Camus, estranged from other people and even from his own deepest self and emotions, is a familiar character in all branches of contemporary writing.

The same kind of loner or outsider, divorced from an uncaring world and pitted by malign fate against it, will be found as the hero, or antihero, of plays by Beckett, Ionesco, Genet and others of lesser talent and renown. The cinematic productions of such directors as Bergman and Fellini portray individuals with disintegrated personalities totally absorbed in themselves and tormented by an intense loneliness and inability to communicate with others.

The theme of alienation has filtered from vanguard circles into popular songs which have reached large segments of youth. Witness these lines from Simon and Garfunkel's *I Am a Rock:*

". . . *I have my books and my poetry to protect me;*
I am shielded in my armor, hiding in my room.
Safe within my womb. I touch no one
And no one touches me.
I am a rock, I am an island.
And a rock can feel no pain:
And an island never cries."*

Millions of less articulate folk share the sentiments of alienation portrayed by so many gifted writers and sen-

---

*Copyright © 1965 by Paul Simon. Used with the permission of Charing Cross Music, Inc.

sitive artists of our day. This is certified by the multitude of sociological studies made of the characteristics of the "lonely crowd," those aggregations of atomized city dwellers who feel crushed and benumbed by the weight of a social system in which they have neither significant purpose nor decision-making power.

The broad attention focused on the condition of alienation shows that we are confronted by the symptoms of a morbid and acute social sickness. The three essays in this book undertake to analyze that endemic condition of capitalism from the Marxist point of view.

Other philosophies also attempt to deal with the problem of alienation from their special standpoints. Existentialism, for example, teaches that alienation is built into the very nature of man as an enigmatic castaway on this planet. Whatever he may do to overcome that state, born of an awareness of the meaninglessness of existence, he can find no exit from his fate.

Marxism on the other hand does not believe in the eternity of alienation any more than it believes in eternal damnation. This state is not an inescapable and irremediable curse of mankind. Alienation is the outgrowth of specific historical conditions which have been brought into existence by man's unwitting activity and which can be changed at a higher stage of economic and social development by man's conscious collective action.

Marxism does agree with existentialism on one point: the tormenting forms of alienation suffered by men and women today disclose extremely significant aspects of their lives which call for a theoretical explanation and a realistic remedy. The method of explanation offered by Marxism for this calamitous condition and the course of action recommended to alleviate it are, however, squarely opposed to the premises and conclusions of either existentialism or any religious creed. Instead of a metaphysical or theological answer, Marxism gives a scientific, an historical materialist analysis of the origins and growth of alienation. It further presents a revolutionary political program for the working class to achieve its reduction and eventual abolition.

Many liberal thinkers view alienation as essentially a

psychological phenomenon. This is a superficial approach. Although alienation has its psychological side — and pathological effects, as Erich Fromm has pointed out in his book *The Sane Society* — it is not primarily or purely of psychic origin and location. Its roots go far back into human history; the causes of its current manifestations are embedded in the innermost constitution of class society.

Alienation is an historically created phenomenon. Its origin and continuing basis in civilized society arises from the alienation of labor which characterizes all systems of private property from slavery to capitalism. Alienation expresses the fact that the creations of men's hands and minds turn against their creators and come to dominate their lives. Thus, instead of enlarging freedom, these uncontrollable powers increase human servitude and strip men of the capacities for self-determination and self-direction which have raised them above the animals.

For Marxism the forms of alienation are products of man's impotence before the forces of nature and of society and his ignorance of the laws of their operation. They are not everlasting. They can diminish to the extent that man's control over his habitat and his social relations and his scientific knowledge of their processes of development are amplified. They will wither away and cease entirely when his command over nature and social organization is consummated under socialism.

The causes of existing alienation are rooted in capitalism which was born and bred in the dispossession of the working masses from the means of production and the consequent alienation of wage labor. In the further course of development this system keeps reproducing the conditions of alienation more extensively on all levels of social existence. Contemporary monopoly capitalism has so intensified and universalized the conditions of alienation that its consequences have spread like an unfilterable virus throughout the whole social organism.

Since alienation in class society is based on the expropriation and exploitation of the labor force, the nature of this deep-seated disease points to the direction of its cure. It can only be eliminated if the unity of the workers with the means of their labor is restored, not by reverting to any form of primitivism, but by incorporating the highest achievements of science, technology and industry into a collectivized mode of production.

This can only be done through a socialist revolution which will establish a regime based upon a nationalized economy operated under the democratic control of the workers themselves. The new world order issuing from such a fundamental reconstruction of human relations can create the conditions for eradicating the forms of alienation inherited from the barbarous past.

Now there are not only capitalist but also postcapitalist countries on this planet. Fourteen workers' states have been established between 1917 and 1973. If alienation is the outcome of capitalist conditions of life and labor, do the phenomena of alienation also exist in these noncapitalist societies? And if so, how are they to be accounted for? What factors are responsible for their recurrence?

For decades Stalin and his successors denied that any sort of alienations could be found in Soviet society; they permitted only "nonantagonistic contradictions" to exist. According to the official mythology, there were occasional frictions and incidental maladjustments, but no serious social tensions or irreconcilable conflicts were possible or observable. Since 1956 the outbursts of opposition in the Soviet bloc, and the assertion of antibureaucratic criticisms despite harsh censorship in the Soviet Union itself, have exposed the reality behind the ideological facade fabricated by the Stalinist apologists.

The problem of the contradictions within the postcapitalist regimes has now become the subject of intense and agonizing inquiry throughout the Communist world. A debate around the question of alienation has been unfolding within intellectual and political circles there for a decade and a half without arriving at any conclusive results.

The theoretical problem is posed in the following terms. Orthodox Marxism taught that alienation is the product of class society and capitalist exploitation. Stalinism asserted that alienation was impossible and absent in the countries which had overthrown capitalist rule. Yet, in defiance of both these positions, malignant manifestations of alienation have cropped up and persist in the countries with a socialist economic base. Why has this happened? How is this discrepancy between the expectations of socialist theory and the facts of life to be explained?

It was logical that Yugoslav intellectuals should raise these questions first and most sharply, because their country was the first to break away from Moscow's monolithic grip. From Yugoslavia the controversy has spread throughout East Europe, except for Albania where the old Stalinist dogmatism — with the added stamp of Mao's endorsement — continues to reign unchallenged.

I shall limit my citations on this point to the foremost Communist philosophers: Georg Lukacs of Hungary, Adam Schaff of Poland, and Roger Garaudy of France. All three have acknowledged, not only that alienation is rife in the workers' states, but also that this fact poses a prime challenge to Marxist theory.

Lukacs has asserted, somewhat paradoxically, that alienation is the most promising of all subjects for Communist writers. This reversal of values which horrifies the guardians of "socialist realism" would have brought harsh penalties down upon him in Stalin's time. The Hungarian critic further advised Communist writers to look at the work of their Western counterparts. "They must learn how the best writers are fighting against alienation. In the end, we shall find political allies among them. It is the task of literature to paint a picture of the enormous alienation that was the product of the Stalinist era, and to help in overcoming it," he said.

Adam Schaff, the leading Polish Communist philosopher and a member of the party's central committee from 1959 until his expulsion from that body in 1968, published a highly controversial book on *Marxism and the Individual* in 1965. In it he propounded the thesis that the abolition of private property does not signify the end of all forms of alienation but only of some of them. "Socialism has not completely overcome any one of the known forms of alienation — not even the economic one," he wrote. Schaff even argues, quite wrongly, that a socialist society will retain certain kinds of alienation because of the complex tasks and extensive administrative apparatus necessarily bound up with the specialization of labor.

Roger Garaudy, long the philosophical bellwether of the French CP and a member of its Politburo, set foot on the road to unorthodoxy in 1963 at an international conference on Franz Kafka held in Czechoslovakia: "What does Kafka tell us today and what makes his work a living thing?" he asked. "Kafka fought against alienation without being able to overcome it. Therefore, Kafka's work is of immediate interest for the capitalist world in which people live in alienation. It is, however, also of immediate interest for the socialist world, because socialism is the beginning of the fight against alienation, for a total man, but it does not abolish all forms of estrangement. As long as the communist society has not been built up, roots of various forms of alienation continue to exist in socialism." Garaudy was finally expelled from the French CP in 1971.

It is understandable why all three of these heterodox thinkers have come into open conflict with the neo-Stalinist bureaucracies in their countries.

It must be considered a big step forward when ideologues of such standing remove the blinders from their eyes and look squarely at the actual alienations which the peoples themselves know only too well. However, up to now, none of the thinkers educated in the school of Stalinism has gone very far in providing a correct elucidation along Marxist lines of the origins and basis of this state of affairs. The essays in this book do undertake such a task of clarification. They indicate what the sources of alienation in the deformed or degenerated workers' states are, and also, in accord with the mandate of Marxism as a guide to action, they point out the ways and means by which these can be removed.

An *autocratic* political structure and a *bureaucratic* management of the economy are the twin pillars of the alienation inflicted on the working masses under the postcapitalist regimes. The prescription for curing these evils can be nothing less than complete democratic control of the government and economy by the workers through their freely elected councils. Such a salutary change from bureaucratic despotism to a socialist democracy is the inevitable next stage of political progress of the workers' states. It has been foreshadowed by the effort of progressive Czechoslovakian Communists to give socialism "a human face" — the effort which was crushed in 1968 by the Kremlin's troops and tanks.

The growing outcries against alienation are directed against the intolerable tyranny of the uncontrolled bureaucracies. The workers along with the intellectuals, youth, and peasants of these countries will have to conquer through their own direct action the full exercise of the democratic rights and rulership which the programs of Marx and Lenin promised but which are denied them under Kosygin and Brezhnev as they were under Stalin and Khrushchev.

GEORGE NOVACK

The Causes of Alienation

by Ernest Mandel

It was by studying Hegel that Marx first came across the concept of alienation. But, oddly enough, it was not the theory of alienated labor that he originally picked up from Hegel's works. It was the alienation of man as a citizen in his relationship with the state that became the starting point of Marx's philosophical, political and social thought.

The social contract theory maintained that in organized society the individual must forfeit a certain number of individual rights to the state as the representative of the collective interest of the community. Hegel especially had developed this idea which was so strongly enunciated by the theoreticians of the natural rights philosophy. That also served as the starting point of Marx's critique of Hegel and his beginning as a critical social thinker in general.

Some small incidents which happened in the Rhine province of western Germany around 1842-43 (the increase in the number of people who stole wood and the intervention of the government against these people) led Marx to conclude that the state, which purports to represent the collective interest, instead represented the interests of only one part of the society, that is to say, those who own

13

private property. Therefore the forfeiture of individual
rights to that state represented a phenomenon of alienation: the loss of rights by people to institutions which
were in reality hostile to them.

Starting from that political-philosophical platform, Marx,
who in the meantime had been expelled from Germany
and had gone into exile in France, got in contact with the
first socialist and workers organizations there and began
to study economics, especially the classical writers of British
political economy, the Adam Smith-Ricardo school. This
was the background for Marx's first attempt in 1844 at
a synthesis of philosophical and economic ideas in the
so-called *Economic and Philosophic Manuscripts of 1844*,
also called the *Parisian Manuscripts*. This was an attempt
to integrate his ideas about labor in bourgeois society
with ideas about the fate of man, man's position in history,
and his existence on earth.

This initial youthful attempt at synthesis was carried out
with very inadequate means. At that period Marx did not
yet have a thorough knowledge of political economy; he
had only started to acquaint himself with some of the basic
notions of the classical school in political economy; and he
had little direct or indirect experience with the modern industrial system. He would obtain all that only during the
next ten years.

This unfinished early work was unknown for a very
long time. It was first published in 1932, nearly one hundred years after it was written. Accordingly, much of the
discussion which had been going on in economic as well
as philosophic circles, about what he thought in his youth
and how he arrived at a certain number of his basic
concepts, was very much distorted by an ignorance of
this specific landmark in his intellectual development.

Immature as parts of it might seem and are, especially
the economic part, it nevertheless represents a major
turning point both in Marx's intellectual development and
in the intellectual history of mankind. Its importance, which
I will try to explain, is linked with the concept of alienation.

Alienation is a very old idea which has religious origins
and is almost as old as organized religion itself. It was

taken over by nearly all the classical philosophical trends
in the West as in the East. This concept turns around
what one could call the tragic fate of man. Hegel, who
was one of the greatest German philosophers, took over
the idea from his predecessors but gave it a new slant
and a new basis which denoted momentous progress. He
did this by changing the foundation of that concept of the
tragic fate of man from a vague anthropological and
philosophical concept into a concept rooted in labor.

Hegel, before Marx, said that man is alienated because
human labor is alienated. He gave two explanations for
this general alienation of human labor. One is what he
called the dialectics of need and labor. Human needs, he
said, are always one step ahead of the available economic
resources; people will therefore always be condemned to
work very hard to fulfill unsatisfied needs. However, the
attempt to equalize the organization of material resources
with the necessity of satisfying all human needs is an
impossible task, a goal which can never be attained.
That was one aspect of what Hegel called alienated labor.

The other side of his philosophical analysis was a bit
more complicated. It is summarized in a difficult word,
the word "externalization" (*Entausserung*). Though the
term is complicated and sounds foreign, its content is
easier to understand. Hegel meant by the philosophical
concept of externalization the fact that every man who
works, who produces something, really reproduces in
his work an idea which he initially had in his head. Some
of you might be astonished if I immediately add that Marx
shared that opinion. You will find this same idea, that
any work which man performs lives in his head before
being realized in material reality, in the first chapter of
Capital. Hegel, as well as Marx, thereby drew a basic
distinction between people and, let us say, ants or other
creatures which seem to be busily at work but do things
purely on instinct. Man, on the other hand, first develops
an idea about what he aims to do and then tries to realize
that idea.

Hegel goes a step farther when he asks, what do we do
in reality when we try to express, in material, what first
lives in us as an idea? We inevitably separate ourselves

from the product of our labor. Anything which we project out of ourselves, anything which we fabricate, anything which we produce, we project out of our own body and it becomes separate from us. It cannot remain as much part and parcel of our being as an idea which continues to live in our head. That was for Hegel the main, let us say, anthropological, definition of alienated labor. He therefore arrived at the conclusion that every and any kind of labor is alienated labor because in any society and under any conditions men will always be condemned to become separated from the products of their labor.

When Marx takes up these two definitions of alienated labor given by Hegel, he contradicts both of them. He says that the discrepancy between needs and material resources, the tension between needs and labor, is a limited one, conditioned by history. It is not true that man's needs can develop in an unlimited way or that the output of his collective labor will always remain inferior to these needs. He denies this most emphatically on the basis of a historical analysis. He especially rejects Hegel's idealistic identification of externalization with alienation. Marx says that when we separate ourselves from the product of our labor it does not necessarily follow that the product of our labor then oppresses us or that any material forces whatsoever turn against men. Such alienation is not the result of the projection of things out of our body as such, which first live in us as ideas and then take on a material existence as objects, as products of our labor.

Alienation results from a certain form of organization of society. More concretely, only in a society which is based on commodity production and only under the specific economic and social circumstances of a market economy, can the objects which we project out of us when we produce acquire a socially oppressive existence of their own and be integrated in an economic and social mechanism which becomes oppressive and exploitative of human beings.

The tremendous advance in human thought which I referred to in this critique of Hegel consists in the fact that Marx rejects the idea of the alienation of labor as being an anthropological characteristic, that is, an inherent and ineradicable curse of mankind. He says that the alienation of labor is not bound to human existence in all places and for all future time. It is a specific result of specific forms of social and economic organization. In other words, Marx transforms Hegel's notion of alienated labor from an eternal anthropological notion into a transitory historical notion.

This reinterpretation carries a message of hope for humanity. Marx says that humanity is not condemned to live "by the sweat of its brow" under alienated conditions throughout its whole term on earth. It can become free, its labor can become free, it is capable of self-emancipation, though only under specific historical conditions. Later I will define what specific social and economic conditions are required for the disappearance of alienated labor.

Let us now pass from the first systematic exposition of his theory of alienation in the *Economic and Philosophic Manuscripts of 1844* to his main work, *Capital*, which was published over twenty years later. It is true that the word alienation hardly appears there.

A new profession has sprung up in the last thirty years which is called "Marxology." Its practitioners read through the works of Marx and put on small index cards all the words he uses in his books and then try to draw some conclusions about his thought from their philological statistics. Some people have even used computers in this type of formal analysis. These "Marx-philologists" have so far discovered six places in *Capital* where the word "alienation" is used either as a noun or as a verb. I certainly will not dispute that colossal discovery though somebody may find a seventh spot or there could be some dispute about the sixth one.

On the basis of such an analysis of *Capital*, done in a purely verbal and superficial way, it could be concluded that the mature Marx did not have a real theory of alienation. Marx would then have discarded it after his youth, after his immature development, especially when, around 1856-57, he became thoroughly convinced of the correctness of the labor theory of value and perfected that labor theory of value himself.

When the *Economic and Philosophic Manuscripts of*

1844 were published for the first time in 1932, a big
controversy arose around these issues. At least three trends
can be distinguished in the debate. I will not cite the names
of all the authors who have participated in it since more
than a hundred people have written on the subject and
the controversy is far from having ended. Some said
there is a contradiction between the youthful and the mature works and Marx abandoned his original theories
when his own views were fully developed.

Others said the opposite. The real Marx is to be found
in the youthful works and he later degenerated by re-
stricting the scope of his understanding to purely economic problems. He thus fell victim to the deviation of
economism.

Still other people tried to deny that Marx's ideas under-
went any significant or substantial evolution whatsoever.
Among these are the American Erich Fromm, the French
Marxist scholar Maximilien Rubel, and two French Catholic priests, Fathers Bigo and Calvez. They maintain
that the same ideas are contained in his early as in his
later works.

I think all three of these opinions are wrong. There
was an important evolution, not an identical repetition,
in Marx's thought from decade to decade. Any person
who thinks, and continues to think and live, will not
say exactly the same thing when he is sixty as when
he was twenty-five. Even if it is conceded that the basic
concepts remain the same, there is obviously some progress, some change. In this concrete case the evolution
is all the more striking, as I said before, because the
Marx of 1844 had not yet accepted the labor theory of
value which is a cornerstone of the economic theory he
developed ten or fifteen years later.

One of the pivotal questions in this continuing debate
is whether the mature Marx held a theory of alienation
or whether he altogether abandoned his original theory
of alienation. This dispute, which can be resolved on
a documentary basis, would not have gone on so long
and inconclusively if it had not been for another unfor-
tunate accident.

It happened that another major work of Marx, *Grun-*

drisse der Kritik der Politischen Okonomie (Fundamental
Outlines of a Critique of Political Economy), a thirteen-
hundred-page work written in 1857-58, which is a kind
of laboratory where all the major ideas of *Capital* were
first elaborated and tested, was also not published until
a century after it was written. Its first publication occurred
at the beginning of the second world war in Russia, but
most of the copies were destroyed as a result of the war.
I believe only two copies arrived in the United States
and none were available in Western Europe. The Rus-
sians under Stalin were not eager to reproduce it a second
time. Thus it was not until the nineteen-fifties, almost
a century after it had been originally written, that the
book was reprinted and became known to a certain number of experts in a few countries.

Unfortunately, only in the last year have portions of
this major work of Marx been translated into English.
It appeared in French only a short time ago. So some
of the participants in this dispute did have the excuse
that they did not know that key work. For anybody
who reads it can at once see that a Marxist theory of
alienation exists because in the *Grundrisse* the word, the
concept, and the analysis appear dozens and dozens of
times.

What then is this theory of alienation as it was developed
by the mature Marx, not by the young Marx? And how
can we relate it to what is set down in *Capital?* There is
first a purely formal difficulty here because Marx uses
three different terms in this connection and he uses them
in an interchangeable manner. One is the concept of alienation; another is the concept of reification, a complicated
word; and a third is the concept of commodity fetishism,
which is still more complicated. However, these three concepts are not so difficult to explain, and I will try to
clarify their meaning for you.

Let us start this analysis with a definition of economic
alienation. I must immediately state that in the comprehensive Marxist theory of alienation, economic alienation is only one part of a much more general phenomenon which covers practically all fields of human activity
in class society. But it is the most decisive element. So

let's start from economic alienation. We will approach it in successive stages. The first and most striking feature of economic alienation is the separation of people from free access to the means of production and means of subsistence. This is a rather recent development in human history. As late as the nineteenth century free access to the means of production in agriculture survived in some countries of the world, among others, in the United States and Canada. Until after the American Civil War it was not impossible for masses of people to find some unpre-empted spot of land and to establish themselves on that acreage as free farmers, as homesteaders. In Europe that possibility had ceased to exist for two hundred years, and in some countries there even three or four hundred years earlier.

That historical factor is the starting point for any theory of alienation because the institution of wage labor in which people are forced to sell their labor power to an-other person, to their employer, can come into existence on a large scale only when and where free access to the means of production and subsistence is denied to an im-portant part of society. Thus the first precondition for the alienation of labor occurs when labor becomes sep-arated from the basic means of production and subsistence.

I said this is a relatively new phenomenon. A second example may illuminate this more sharply. The classical historical criticism made by liberal thought in the nine-teenth century about the society of the middle ages, feudal society, was the lack of freedom of the cultivators of the soil. I won't take exception to that criticism which I think was correct. The direct producers in that society, the peas-ants and serfs, were not free people. They could not move about freely; they were tied to the land.

But what the bourgeois liberal critics of feudal society forgot was that tying people to the land was a two-sided phenomenon. If a person was tied to the land, the land was also tied to the person. And because the land was tied to the person there wasn't any important part of the people living within feudal relations who could be forced to become wage laborers and sell their labor power to owners of capital. They had access to the land, they could produce their own means of subsistence and keep part of it for themselves. Only people outside organized feudal society, in reality outlaws, because that is what they were originally, could become the starting point for new social classes — wage laborers on the one hand, merchants on the other.

The second stage in the alienation of labor came about when part of society was driven off the land, no longer had access to the means of production and means of subsistence, and, in order to survive, was forced to sell its labor power on the market. That is the main characteristic of alienated labor. In the economic field it is the institution of wage labor, the economic obligation of people who cannot otherwise survive to sell the only commodity they possess, their labor power, on the labor market.

What does it mean to sell your labor power to a boss? In Marx's analysis, both in his youthful and his mature work, behind this purely formal and legal contractual relation — you sell your labor power, part of your time, to another for money to live on — is in reality something of deepgoing consequence for all human existence and particularly for the life of the wage laborer. It first of all implies that you lose control over a large part of your waking hours. All the time which you have sold to the employer belongs to him, not to you. You are not free to do what you want at work. It is the employer who dictates what you will and will not do during this whole time. He will dictate what you produce, how you produce it, where you produce it. He will be master over your activity.

And the more the productivity of labor increases and the shorter the workweek becomes, the stricter will be the control of the employer over every hour of your time as a wage laborer. In time and motion studies — the ultimate and most perfected form of this control — the boss even tries to control every second, *literally* every second, of the time which you spend in his employ.

Alienation thereupon acquires a third form. When a wage earner has sold his labor power for a certain part of his life to his employer, the products of his labor are not his own. The products of his labor become the property of the employer.

The fact that the modern wage earner owns none of the products of his own labor, obvious as it may appear to people who are accustomed to bourgeois society, is not at all so self-evident from the viewpoint of human history as a whole. It was not like that for thousands upon thousands of years of human existence. Both the medieval handicraftsman and the handicraftsman of antiquity were the proprietors of their own products. The peasant, and even the serf of the middle ages, remained in possession of at least 50 per cent, sometimes 60 and 70 per cent, of the output of their own labor.

Under capitalism not only does the wage earner lose possession of the product of his labor, but these products can function in a hostile and injurious manner against him. This happened with the machine. This remarkable product of human ingenuity becomes a source of tyranny against the worker when the worker serves as an appendage of the machine and is forced to adapt the cadence of his life and work to the operation of the machine. This can become a serious source of alienation in shift work when part of the working class has to work during the night or at odd hours in conflict with the normal rhythm of human life between day and night. Such an abnormal schedule causes all sorts of psychological and nervous disorders.

Another aspect of the oppressive nature which the products of labor can acquire once society is divided into hostile classes of capitalists and wage workers are the crises of overproduction, depressions or, as it is nowadays more prudently put, recessions. Then people consume less because they produce too much. And they consume less, not because their labor is inadequately productive, but because their labor is too productive.

We come now to a final form of alienated labor in the economic field which derives from the conclusions of the points I have noted. The alienation of the worker and his labor means that something basic has changed in the life of the worker. What is it? Normally everybody has some creative capacity, certain talents lodged in him, untapped potentialities for human development which should be expressed in his labor activity.

However, once the institution of wage labor is prevalent, these possibilities become nullified. Work is no longer a means of self-expression for anybody who sells his labor time. Work is just a means to attain a goal. And that goal is to get money, some income to be able to buy the consumer goods necessary to satisfy your needs.

In this way a basic aspect of human nature, the capacity to perform creative work, becomes thwarted and distorted. Work becomes something which is not creative and productive for human beings but something which is harmful and destructive. Catholic priests and Protestant pastors who have worked in factories in Western Europe, the so-called "worker-priests," who have written books about their experiences, have arrived at conclusions on this point that are absolutely identical with those of Marxism. They declare that a wage earner considers the hours passed in factories or in offices as time lost from his life. He must spend time there in order to get freedom and capacity for human development outside the sphere of production and of work.

Ironically, this hope for fulfillment during leisure time turns out to be an illusion. Many humanitarian and philanthropic reformers of liberal or social-democratic persuasion in the nineteenth and the beginning of the twentieth centuries thought that men could become liberated when their leisure time would increase. They did not understand that the nature of leisure was likewise determined by the nature of wage labor and by the conditions of a society based on commodity production and wage labor.

Once socially necessary labor time became shorter and leisure time greater, a commercialization of leisure took place. The capitalist society of commodity production, the so-called "consumer society" did its utmost to integrate leisure time into the totality of economic phenomena at the basis of commodity production, exploitation and accumulation.

At this point the notion of alienation is extended from a purely economic to a broader social phenomenon. The first bridge to this wider application is the concept of alienation of the consumer. Thus far we have spoken only about the consequences of alienated labor. But one of the cardinal characteristics of capitalist society, as Marx understood as early as 1844, is its built-in contradiction regarding human needs. On the one hand, each capitalist entrepreneur tries to limit the human needs of his own wage earners as much as possible by paying as little wages as possible. Otherwise he would not make enough profit to accumulate.

On the other hand, each capitalist sees in the work force of all the other capitalists not wage earners but potential consumers. He would therefore like to expand the capacity of consumption of these other wage earners to the limit or otherwise he cannot increase production and sell what his own workers produce. Thus capitalism has a tendency to constantly extend the needs of people.

Up to a certain point this expansion can cover genuine human needs, such as the elementary requirements of feeding, housing and clothing everybody in more or less decent circumstances. Very quickly, however, capitalism in its efforts to commercialize everything and sell as many gadgets as possible, goes beyond any rational human needs and starts to spur and stimulate artificial needs in a systematic, large-scale manner. Some of these are absurd and grotesque. Let me give one example. An American author, Jessica Mitford, has written an amusing book, called *The American Way of Death*. It describes the practices of morticians who seek to induce people to buy more expensive coffins so that the beloved dead can rest not only peacefully, but lightly, on foam mattresses. The sales pitchmen say this satisfies, not the corpse, but the feelings of the consumer.

Is it necessary to observe that no real need is involved in this grotesque attempt of the burial business to make money? It is scandalous to feed in this mercenary manner upon the feelings of grief of people who have lost members of their family.

Such alienation is no longer purely economic but has become social and psychological in nature. For what is the motivation of a system for constantly extending needs beyond the limits of what is rational? It is to create, purposely and deliberately, permanent and meretricious dissatisfactions in human beings. Capitalism would cease to exist if people were fully and healthily satisfied. The system must provoke continued artificial dissatisfaction in human beings because without that dissatisfaction the sales of new gadgets which are more and more divorced from genuine human needs cannot be increased.

A society which is turned toward creating systematic frustration of this kind generates the bad results recorded in the crime pages of the daily newspapers. A society which breeds worthless dissatisfaction will also breed all kinds of antisocial attempts to overcome this dissatisfaction.

Beyond this alienation of human beings as consumers, there are two very important aspects of alienation. One is the alienation of human activity in general. The other is the alienation of human beings in one of their most fundamental features, the capacity to communicate.

What is meant by the extension of the concept of alienation to human activity in general? We live in a society based on commodity production and a social division of labor pushed to the limits of overspecialization. As a result, people in a particular job or doing a certain type of activity for a living will incline to have an extremely narrow horizon. They will be prisoners of their trade, seeing only the problems and preoccupations of their specialty. They will also tend to have a restricted social and political awareness because of this limitation.

Along with this shut-in horizon will go something which is much worse, the tendency to transform relations between human beings into relations between things. This is that famous tendency toward "reification," the transformation of social relations into things, into objects, of which Marx speaks in *Capital*.

This way of looking at phenomena is an extension of this theory of alienation. Here is an example of this transformation which I witnessed the other day in this country. The waiters and waitresses in restaurants are poor working people who are the victims and not the authors of this process of reification. They are even unaware of the nature of their involvement in this phenom-

enon. While they are under heavy pressure to serve the
maximum number of customers on the job imposed upon
them by the system and its owners, they look upon the
customers solely under the form of the orders they put
in. I heard one waitress address herself to a person and
say, "Ah, you are the corned-beef and cabbage." You
are not Mr. or Mrs. Brown, not a person of a certain
age and with a certain address. You are "corned-beef
and cabbage" because the waitress has on her mind the
orders taken under stress from so many people.

This habit of reification is not the fault of the inhu-
manity or insensitivity of the workers. It results from
a certain type of human relation rooted in commodity
production and its extreme division of labor where people
engaged in one trade tend to see their fellows only as
customers or through the lenses of whatever economic
relations they have with them.

This outlook finds expression in everyday language.
I have been told that in the city of Osaka, the main com-
mercial and industrial capital of Japan, the common mode
of addressing people when you meet is not "how do you
do?" but "how is business?" or "are you making money?"
This signifies that bourgeois economic relations have so
completely pervaded ordinary human relations as to de-
humanize them to an appreciable extent.

I now come to the ultimate and most tragic form of
alienation, which is alienation of the capacity to communicate. The capacity to communicate has become the
most fundamental attribute of man, of his quality as
a human being. Without communication, there can be
no organized society because without communication, there
is no language, and without language, there is no intelligence. Capitalist society, class society, commodity-producing society tends to thwart, divert and partially destroy
this basic human capacity.

Let me give three examples of this process at three
different levels, starting with a most commonplace case.
How do people learn to communicate? While they are
infants they go through what psychologists call a process of socialization and learn to speak. For a long time
one of the main methods of socializing young children

has been through playing with dolls. When children play with dolls, they duplicate themselves, project themselves outside their own individuality, and carry on a dialogue with that other self. They speak two languages, their own language and the language of the doll, thereby bringing into play an artificial process of communication which, through its spontaneous nature, facilitates the development of language and intelligence.

Recently, industry started to produce dolls which speak. This is supposed to be a mark of progress. But once the doll speaks, the dialogue is limited. The child no longer speaks in two languages, or with the same spontaneity. Part of its speech is induced, and induced by some capitalist corporation.

That corporation may have hired the biggest educators and psychologists who make the doll speak more perfectly than any of the babble which could come out of the child's mind itself — although I have some doubts on that subject. Nevertheless, the spontaneous nature of the dialogue is partially thwarted, suppressed or detoured. There is less development of dialogue, of capacity for communication, and therefore a lesser formation of intelligence than in more backward times when dolls did not speak and children had to give them a language of their own.

A second example is taken from a more sophisticated level. Any class society which is divided by social-material interests and in which class struggle goes on suppresses to a certain extent the capacity for communication between people standing on different sides of the barricades. This is not a matter of lack of intelligence, of understanding or honesty, from any individual point of view. This is simply the effect of the inhibitive pressures that substantial divisive material interests exercise on any group of individuals.

Anybody who has ever been present at wage bargaining where there is severe tension between workers' and employers' representatives — I'm talking about real wage bargaining, not sham wage bargaining — will understand what I am referring to. The employers' side simply cannot sympathize with or understand what the workers are talk-

ing about even if they have the utmost good will and
liberal opinions, because their material-social interests prevent them from understanding what the other side is most
concerned with.

There was a very striking example of this inhibition
on another level (because workers and not employers
were involved) in the tragic strike of the United Federa-
tion of Teachers in New York in 1968 against the decentralization of control over the school system. People
of bad will, fools or stupid people were not so much
involved. Indeed, most of them would have been called
liberal or even left some time ago. But through very strong
pressures of social interest and social milieu, they were
simply incapable of understanding what the other side,
the Black and Puerto Rican masses who wanted community control over the education of their children, was
talking about.

Thus the Marxist notion of alienation extends far beyond the oppressed classes of society, properly speaking.
The oppressors are also alienated from part of their human capacity through their inability to communicate on
a human basis with the majority of society. And this
divorcement is inevitable as long as class society and
its deep differentiations exist.

Another terrible expression of this alienation on the
individual scale is the tremendous loneliness which a society based on commodity production and division of
labor inevitably induces in many human beings. Ours
is a society based on the principle, every man for himself.
Individualism pushed to the extreme also means loneliness pushed to the extreme.

It is simply not true, as certain existentialist philosophers contend, that man has always been an essentially
lonely human being. There have been forms of integrated
collective life in primitive society where the very notion
of loneliness could not arise. It arises out of commodity
production and division of labor only at a certain stage
of human development in bourgeois society. And then
unfortunately it acquires a tremendous extension which
can go beyond the limits of mental health.

Psychologists have gone around with tape recorders
and listened to certain types of dialogues between people

in shops or on the street. When they play these dialogues afterwards they discover that there has been no exchange whatsoever. The two people have talked along parallel lines without once meeting with each other. Each talks because he welcomes the occasion to unburden himself, to get out of his loneliness, but he is incapable of listening to what the other person is saying.

The only meeting place is at the end of the dialogue when they say goodbye. Even that farewell is saddening because they want to save the possibility of unburdening themselves of their loneliness the next time they meet. They carry on what the French call *dialogue de sourds,* dialogues between deaf people, that is, dialogues between people who are incapable of understanding or listening to other people.

This is of course an extreme and marginal illustration. Happily, the majority of members of our society are not yet in that situation or otherwise we would be on the brink of a complete breakdown of social relations. Nonetheless, capitalism tends to extend the zone of this extreme loneliness with all its terrible implications.

This looks like a very dim picture, and the dim picture undoubtedly corresponds to the dim reality of our times. If the curve of mental sickness has climbed parallel with the curve of material wealth and income in most of the advanced countries of the West, this dismal picture has not been invented by Marxist critics but corresponds to very deep-rooted aspects of the social and economic reality in which we live.

But, as I said before, this grim situation is not at all without hope. Our optimism comes from the fact that, after all this analysis of the roots of the alienation of labor and the specific expressions of the alienation of man in bourgeois society is completed, there emerges the inescapable conclusion that a society can be envisaged in which there will be no more alienation of labor and alienation of human beings. This is a historically produced and man-made evil, not an evil rooted in nature or human nature. Like everything else which has been made by man, it can also be unmade by man. This condition is a product of history and it can be destroyed by history or at least gradually overcome by further progress.

Thus the Marxist theory of alienation implies and con-
tains a theory of disalienation through the creation of
conditions for the gradual disappearance and eventual
abolition of alienation. I stress "gradual disappearance"
because such a process or institution can no more be
abolished by fiat or a stroke of the pen than commodity
production, the state, or the division of society into classes
can be eliminated by a government decree or proclamation.

Marxists understand that the social and economic pre-
conditions for a gradual disappearance of alienation can
be brought about only in a classless society ushered in by
a world socialist revolution. And when I say a classless
socialist society, I obviously do not mean the societies
which exist in the Soviet Union, Eastern Europe or China.
In the best cases these are transitional societies somewhere
halfway between capitalism and socialism. Though private
property has been abolished, they have not yet abolished
the division of society into classes, they still have different
social classes and different social layers, division of labor
and commodity production. As a consequence of these
conditions, they still have alienated labor and alienated
men.

The prerequisites for the disappearance of human alienation, of alienated labor and the alienated activities of
human beings, can only be created precisely through
the continuation of those processes I have just named:
the withering away of commodity production, the disappearance of economic scarcity, the withering away of
social division of labor through the disappearance of
private ownership of the means of production and the
elimination of the difference between manual and intellectual
labor, between producers and administrators. All of this
would bring about the slow transformation of the very
nature of labor from a coercive necessity in order to
get money, income and means of consumption into a
voluntary occupation that people want to do because it
covers their own internal needs and expresses their talents.
This transformation of labor into all-sided creative human
activity is the ultimate goal of socialism. Only when that
goal is attained will alienated labor and all its pernicious
consequences cease to exist.

Progressive Disalienation through the Building of Socialist Society, or the Inevitable Alienation in Industrial Society?

by Ernest Mandel

The ideological and mystificating distortion of the Marxist theory of alienation has specific social sources in the reality of our time. Furthermore, it fulfills obvious apologetic functions. The ideologists of the bourgeoisie try to present the most repulsive features of contemporary capitalism as eternal and inevitable results of the "human drama." They endeavor to reduce the socio-historical conception of human alienation to an anthropological conception, bearing the mark of resignation and despair. As for the Stalinist ideologists, they strive to reduce the "valid kernel" of the theory of alienation to specific features of the *capitalist* exploitation of labor, in order to "prove" that alienation no longer exists in the Soviet Union and cannot exist in any society in transition from capitalism to socialism (nor, *a fortiori*, in any socialist society).

Conversely, the glaring survival of phenomena of alienation in Soviet society serves as a basis for bourgeois ideologists to demonstrate triumphantly the absolute inevitability of alienation "in industrial society." And the obstinacy with which official Soviet ideology denies the evidence—that is, the survival of phenomena of alienation during the transition from capitalism to socialism—risks eliciting similar conclusions from Marxist theoreticians in countries with a socialist economic basis who are sincerely seeking to discover the reality under the veil of official lies.

An analysis of the Marxist theory of alienation is thus incomplete as long as it does not enable one to formulate a *Marxist theory of progressive disalienation* and does not defend this successfully against the myth of "inevitable alienation" in any and every "industrial society."

A Marxist concept of alienation and disalienation clearly does not fit in with the apologetic assertions of writers like Jahn, according to whom "the domination of an alien power over men is done away with when private property is abolished by the proletarian revolution and the building of communist society, since here men find themselves freely facing their own products . . ." [1] A similar view is upheld by Manfred Buhr, who writes that alienation is "eliminated only with the socialist revolution and the formation of the dictatorship of the proletariat, in the process of building socialist society." [2] The author adds, to be sure, that all the phenomena of alienation do not vanish spontaneously on the morrow of the socialist revolution. But he refers in this connection to vague ideological and psychological "survivals" from the capitalist era, bourgeois individualism and egoism, without revealing their material and social roots.

In a later work, Buhr declares quite clearly: "Just as the social phenomenon of alienation is a phenomenon of historical origin and will cease to manifest itself as history advances, the concept of alienation that reflects it is likewise an historical concept and cannot be applied significantly to any but capitalist conditions." [3] There is obviously no causal relationship between the first and second parts of this sentence. The fact that alienation is an histor-

---

1. Wolfgang Jahn, "Der ökonomische Inhalt des Begriffs der Entfremdung der Arbeit in den Frühschriften von Karl Marx," *Wirtschaftswissenschaft*, no. 6 (1957). p. 864.

2. Manfred Buhr, "Entfremdung," in *Philosophisches Wörterbuch*, Georg Klaus and Manfred Buhr, eds., (Leipzig, 1964). p. 140. It must be emphasized that, despite this weakness regarding the problem of disalienation, Buhr's text represents an advance over the way the question of alienation had previously been dealt with in the German Democratic Republic.

3. Buhr, "Entfremdung — Philosophische Anthropologie — Marx-Kritik," *Deutsche Zeitschrift für Philosophie*, 14th year, no. 7 (Berlin, 1966). p. 814. In a footnote, Buhr admits that disalienation is a *process* which merely *begins* with the over-

ically limited phenomenon does not in the least imply that its validity is limited to the capitalist epoch alone.

T. I. Oiserman expounds his argument on a higher plane: "Under socialism [the writer here refers explicitly to the "first phase of socialism," defined by Marx in *The Critique of the Gotha Programme*] what Marx called the essence, the content, of alienation does not exist and, in the strict sense, it cannot exist under socialism: this content being the domination of the producers by the products of their labor, alienation of productive activity, alienated social relations, subjection of the personality to the spontaneous forces of social evolution." [4]

Unfortunately, all the phenomena Oiserman lists not only can survive in the epoch of transition from capitalism to socialism, but they even survive *inevitably*, in so far as commodity production, the exchange of labor power for a strictly limited and calculated wage, the *economic obligation* to effect this exchange, the division of labor (and in particular the division of labor between manual work and mental work, and so on), continue to survive. In a transitional society which is bureaucratically distorted or degenerated, these phenomena may even acquire greater and greater scope.

This is clear from an analysis in depth of the economic reality of the countries with a socialized economic basis. It is plain that the workers' needs as consumers are not at all completely met: does that not imply alienation of the worker in relation to the products of his labor, especially when these products are goods he wants to obtain, and the inadequate development of the productive forces (not to mention the bureaucratic distortion of the distributive system!) prevents him from doing so? It is also plain that the division of labor (the negative effects of which are reinforced

---

throw of capitalist society. But he concludes that it is not possible to deduce from these premises that phenomena of alienation are still to be found in socialist society (more precisely, in the epoch of transition from capitalism to socialism). Everything in socialism that is referred to "commonly and carelessly" as alienation is at most only "externally similar" to capitalist alienation. The apologetic aspect of this casuistry stares one in the face.

4. T. I. Oiserman, *Die Entfremdung als historische Kategorie*, (Berlin, 1965). p. 135.

by the bureaucratic organization of the economy) often alienates
the worker and citizen from productive activity. The number of
candidates for university places who are not accepted and who are
therefore compelled to engage in activities whose *sole purpose is
to earn a living* are so many witnesses to this alienation. One could
add to the list indefinitely. In Czechoslovakia a Communist writer
named Miroslav Kusy has not hesitated to draw attention to the
new phenomena of alienation caused by the bureaucratization of
institutions which alienate themselves from the people.[5] This is a
subject that could be developed at great length. Even a writer
as subtle as J. N. Dawydow prefers to ignore this problem and
prudently restricts himself to an analysis of the conditions of disalienation in the second phase of socialism—a noteworthy analysis,
to which I shall return later.

Under these conditions one can only applaud Henri Lefebvre
when he states flatly that "Marx never restricted the sphere of
alienation to capitalism." [6] And one must acknowledge the cour-
age of Wolfgang Heise when he declares: "Overcoming alienation
is identical with the development of the conscious socialist individual and the collective power to create. It is realized through
the building of socialism and communism. Thus it is an aspect of
the whole historical process whereby the marks of the old society
are overcome in all the relations and activities of life. It begins
with the emancipation of the working class, the struggle for the
dictatorship of the proletariat, *and ends with the realization of
social self-management in its most complete form.*" [7] This seems to
me broadly correct, even if we must criticize Heise for his analysis
of the *concrete* aspects of alienation and of the process of disalienation in the epoch of transition from capitalism to socialism.

In any case, this point must be kept firmly in mind: for Marx,
the phenomenon of alienation is older than capitalism. It is con-
nected with the inadequate development of the productive forces,

---

5. Quoted by Gunther Hillmann in "Zum Verständnis der
Texte," *Karl Marx, Texte zu Methode und Praxis, II, Pariser
Manuskripte* 1844, (Hamburg, 1966). pp. 216-217.

6. Henri Lefebvre, Preface to the second edition of *Critique
de la Vie quotidienne*, Vol. I, (Paris, 1958). p. 74.

7. Wolfgang Heise, "Uber die Entfremdung und ihre
Uberwindung," *Deutsche Zeitschrift fur Philosophie*, no. 6 (Berlin, 1965). p. 701.

with commodity production, money economy, and the social division of labor. As long as these phenomena continue to exist, the survival of human alienation in some form or other is inevitable.[8]

The Yugoslav Communist theoretician Boris Ziherl admits its existence in "socialist society" (I should call it, more correctly, society in transition from capitalism to socialism), and this is entirely to his credit. But he does this only to remonstrate with those Yugoslav philosophers who call for beginning disalienation by beginning the withering away of the commodity economy, or who lay emphasis on the unnecessary and alienating forms of constraint that continue to exist in Yugoslav society.[9]

The position of the official Yugoslav theoreticians on this question is highly contradictory. They say that material conditions are not ripe for the withering away of the commodity economy and the alienation that results from it. But are material conditions ripe for the withering away of the state? In their struggle against Stalin and his followers, the Yugoslav Communists appealed to Lenin who had shown in *State and Revolution* that in order to conform with the advance toward socialism the withering away of the state must begin "on the day after the proletarian revolution," that the proletariat must build a state "which is no longer a state in the strict sense of the word." They proclaimed, and rightly, that refusal to take this road, far from preparing "the maturation of objective conditions," would inevitably set up *extra obstacles* in the way of a future withering away, which could not, after all, develop out of a constant reinforcement of the same state!

But this reasoning, which is correct as it applies to the state, is equally correct in relation to commodity economy.[10] The proletariat cannot deprive itself of this immediately after the overthrow

---

8. A variant of the apologetic conception is offered by E. V. Ilenkov, who says that only "the antagonistic division of labor," "the bourgeois division of labor," has the effect of mutilating man. (*La dialettica dell 'astratto e del concreto nel Capitale di Marx*, Milan, 1961, p. 32). For Marx, *all* division of labor that condemns man to do one job only — and therefore the division of labor that continues to exist in the USSR — is alienating.

9. Boris Ziherl, "On the Objective and Subjective Conditions of Disalienation Under Socialism, in *Socialist Thought and Practice* (Yugoslavia), January-March 1965. pp. 122, 129-130.

10. Heise ("Uber die Entfremdung," pp. 700-711) analyzes

of capitalism; it is linked with a historical phase in the development of the productive forces which has far from been outgrown in what are called the "developing" countries (and all the countries with a socialized economic basis, except the German Democratic Republic, were in this category when they began to build socialism). The state can and must be used, within the framework of a planned economy, in order to perfect the planning of the economy and hasten the development of the productive forces, without which its ultimate withering away would be a utopian prospect.

At the same time, however, it must *begin to wither away* or its extension will create fresh obstacles, both objective and subjective, in the path of its future withering away. The nature of these fresh obstacles is revealed in tragic fashion in Yugoslavia, where the commodity has produced a social contradiction whose principle it harbors, namely, unemployment, with all the consequences that also follow for man's consciousness.[11] No more can the state miraculously wither away all at once after being constantly reinforced in the preceding period than can the commodity economy miraculously wither away after being constantly consolidated and extended in the period of transition between capitalism and socialism.

The Yugoslav philosophers who bring up the problem of the survival and reproduction of phenomena of alienation in their

---

in detail a number of factors which hold back the process of disalienation during the phase of the building of socialism — in reality, the phase of transition from capitalism to socialism. But he does not even mention, in this context, the survival of commodity economy and money economy, though this is one of the essential sources of alienation, according to Marx!

11. Completely forgetting the connection between alienation and commodity production, the Yugoslav economist Branko Horvat sees the road leading to the abolition of alienation in self-management. He writes: "Control of production without the state as intermediary means control by direct producers, which in turn means that the equality of proletarians is turned into the equality of masters. The process of human alienation . . . comes to an end . . . (*Toward a Theory of Economic Planning*, Belgrade, 1964, p. 80.) Strange "masters" indeed, who may find themselves on the street, without work or income worthy of the name!

country[12] are thus more "Marxist" in relation to this problem than the official theoreticians—even if they are sometimes led, under the influence of their own bad experiences, to put a question mark over the Marxist theory of the complete disalienation of man in communist society. The possibility of this disalienation is also challenged in two recent works by Henri Lefebvre[13] in which the author can see nothing more than a continual swinging to and fro between alienation, disalienation, and re-alienation. He says, rightly, that it is necessary "fully to particularize," "historicize," and "relativize" the concept of alienation.[14] If, though, in relativizing this concept we do away with the possibility of completely negating it, we tend to make it absolute again. Thus, Lefebvre's attempt to "historicize" alienation must be regarded as a failure, since it has produced the opposite dialectical result, transforming alienation into a concept which is immanent in human society, even if it presents itself in a different form in each type of society.

The sources of this historical skepticism are obvious: they are the negative phenomena that have accompanied the first historical endeavors to build a socialist society[15]—the results of Stalinism—which have outrageously and uselessly intensified the phenomena

---

12. I will mention, among others: Rudi Supek, "Dialectique de la pratique sociale," in *Praxis*, No. 1, 1965; Gajo Petrović, "Marx's Theory of Alienation," and also "Man as Economic Animal and Man as Praxis," in *Inquiry*, 1963; Predrag Vranicki, "Socialism and the Problem of Alienation," in *Praxis*, No. 2-3, 1965, and "La signification actuelle de l'humanisme du jeune Marx," in *Annali dell'Istituto Giangiacomo Feltrinelli*, 1964-1965; Zaga Pesić-Golubović, "What Is the Meaning of Alienation?" in *Praxis*, No. 5, 1966.

13. Lefebvre, *Critique de la Vie quotidienne*, Vol. II, (Paris, 1961) and *Introduction à la modernité* (Paris, 1962).

14. *Critique de la Vie quotidienne*, Vol. II, p. 209.

15. "*Today* we are less convinced than Marx was that there can be an absolute end to alienation." (Lefebvre, *Introduction à la modernité*, p. 146. Emphasis mine. — E. M.) By referring to *present-day* conditions in order to justify this conclusion, Lefebvre seems to forget the premises of Marx's argument: the withering away of commodity production, money economy, and the social division of labor, on a world scale, and on the basis of a very high level of development of productive forces.

of alienation and which cannot but continue to exist in the period of transition from capitalism to socialism.

Thus, the neo-skepticism of a Lefebvre or of a Pesić-Golubović is only a negative reaction in face of the Stalinist experience, just as the apologetic writing of Buhr, Jahn, Oiserman, and Ilenkov is only a product of the same experience, an attempt to gloss over the negative aspects of social reality in the countries with a socialized economic basis. Once thinking outgrows apologetics of this sort, in a new political context in Eastern Europe, it may either take the path of a return to the original conception of disalienation as we find it in Marx—disalienation conceived of as a process depending on a material and social infrastructure which does not yet exist in the period of transition from capitalism to socialism—or else the path of skepticism about the possibility of complete disalienation.

But the task for scientific thought is to analyze the social and economic sources of the continued existence of phenomena of alienation during the period of transition between capitalism and socialism and during the first phase of socialism, and to discover the driving forces of the process of disalienation during these historical phases. This means undertaking an analysis that begins by putting aside those factors reinforcing and aggravating alienation as a result of the bureaucratic distortion or degeneration of a society in transition, and then later on integrating these special factors in a more concrete analysis of the phenomena of alienation in countries like the U.S.S.R., the "people's democracies," and so on.

The general source of the continued existence of phenomena of alienation during the transition period and in the first phase of socialism is the inadequate level of development of the productive forces and the resulting survival of bourgeois norms of distribution.[16] The contradiction between the socialized mode of production and the bourgeois norms of distribution—the chief contradiction of the transition period—brings factors of alienation into production relations. The workers continue to suffer, even if only partially, from the effects of an objective and elemental social

---

16. See the expression used by Marx in *Critique of the Gotha Programme*, in *Selected Works*, Vol. III, pp. 19-20. See also my *Marxist Economic Theory*, Vol. II, (New York, 1969), p. 565.

evolution which they do not control (the survival of the "laws of the market" in the sphere of consumer goods; the survival of a selection procedure for jobs which does not permit full development of all the aptitudes of every individual, etc.).

When to *these* circumstances we add the hypertrophy of bureaucracy, the lack of socialist democracy on the political level, the lack of workers' self-management on the economic plane, the lack of freedom to create on the cultural plane, *specific factors of alienation* resulting from bureaucratic distortion or degeneration are added to the inevitable factors mentioned in the previous paragraph. The bureaucratization of the transitional society tends to aggravate the contradiction between the socialized mode of production and the bourgeois norms of distribution, particularly by intensifying social inequality. The generalization of a money economy works in the same way.

Wolfgang Heise makes a very subtle analysis of this problem. While collective ownership of the means of production and socialist planning *in principle* overcome social helplessness in relation to the evolution of society as a whole, this does not mean that this social helplessness is immediately overcome for every individual. It is necessary to take into account not only the ideological slag of the capitalist past, of the members of the former ruling classes who are still around, of the inadequate level of education of part of the proletariat, and so on; we have also to realize that this helplessness is overcome in practice only when individuals *realize* their identity with society through social activity based on a large number of free decisions.[17] This implies not only complete self-management by labor at the level of the economy taken as a whole (not merely in the production process but also in distribution and consumption), but also a withering away of the state and the disappearance of all human relationships based on constraint and oppression.

Thus far, Heise's analysis seems to me to be correct. But in stating that the process of disalienation cannot be a spontaneous phenomenon but must be guided by the Party, he begins by saying that the risk of bureaucratization—of seeing the machinery of government become independent in relation to the purposes of society as a whole—can best be neutralized by Party action.[18] This

17. Heise, "Uber die Entfremdung," pp. 702-703.
18. Ibid., p. 704.

is to take an idealistic view and lose sight of the fact that there are *two objective sources* of bureaucratization: on the one hand, the survival of spontaneous economic processes (the survival of norms of commodity distribution and of elements of a commodity economy, the survival of the division of labor, of cultural privileges, and of delegations of authority, all of which cause the machinery of government to become independent and transform itself from the servant into the master of society), and, on the other hand, the centralization of the social surplus product and the right to dispose of it freely that belongs to the state machine. The dual process of disalienation in relation to these specific phenomena of alienation thus consists in the progressive withering away of the commodity economy and of social inequality and the replacement of the system of state management of the economy by a system of workers' self-management, democratically centralized. Thereby the material infrastructure of bureaucratization is destroyed, and it is only under these conditions that the subjective activity of the Party—and the broadening of socialist democracy on the political plane, which implies abandonment of the dogma of the single party—can be freed from the bureaucratic grip which subjugates it.[19]

Heise rightly insists on the importance of a sufficient level of development of the productive forces in order to make possible the unleashing of all these processes of disalienation. However, after having first sinned by voluntarism, he goes on to sin by a mechanistic deviation. Such a development of the productive forces demands "an extraordinarily high level of organization and differentiation of social functions"; for this reason it would be "senseless to demand direct democracy in production or the abandonment of authoritarian central planning . . . as a condition for overcoming alienation. . . . This would be a demand running counter to the real needs of rational production, to economic and technical logic . . ." [20]

It is noteworthy that, when pushed back into its last entrenchments, an apologia for the lack of workers' self-management in the German Democratic Republic makes use of the same argument—"the high level of differentiation of social functions"—

19. It is well known that in the USSR in Stalin's time the Party was the chief vehicle of bureaucratization.

20. Heise, "Uber die Entfremdung," p. 706.

used by bourgeois ideologists to show that alienation is inevitable, not merely under capitalism but in any "industrial society." I shall come back to this point later. It is also noteworthy that Heise cannot conceive of central planning except as authoritarian planning and that, like the Yugoslav writers already mentioned, he remains caught in a dilemma: either anarchy of production (market economy) or authoritarian planning. The possibility of *democratically centralized* planning, the outcome of a congress of workers' councils managing the enterprises, seems to elude him. What he calls "the lowering of the level of organization of society" means for him (as for the Stalinist and bourgeois writers) the abolition of authoritarian structures. As if the "associated producers," to use Marx's expression, were incapable of raising the level of social *organization* by substituting, at least among themselves,[21] freely accepted discipline for a hierarchy of persons giving and receiving orders!

But the basic weakness of Heise's argument lies still deeper. On the one hand, he appeals to the primacy of Party activity (against tendencies both to spontaneity and to bureaucracy); on the other, he invokes the primacy of economic growth (against democratizing the life of the enterprises). He does not seem to realize that the power of the bureaucracy is reflected *subjectively* in this economic argument, and that by accepting it one paralyzes in advance any subjective activity directed against the bureaucracy. For does not the latter claim to personify "competence" and "specialization" as against the ignorant masses? Nor does Heise notice that *objectively* the bureaucracy remains all powerful as long as it can dispose with sovereign authority of the social surplus product (whether by way of the authority it possesses, as in the U.S.S.R., or through the medium of the "laws of the market," as in Yugoslavia).

This is why he calls for plenty of "correctives" to "mistakes," in the form of an "increasing right of control by the community"; this is why he recognizes that in the long run the centralization of authority in the state machine must be overcome by "socialist democracy" and the "development of conscious activity by the

---

21. Coercion obviously continues to be inevitable where other social classes are concerned, but the degree of this coercion depends on the violence of social contradictions.

masses" [22]—but without drawing what is from the Marxist stand-
point the obvious conclusion, namely that the decisive step toward
this democracy is one which subjects the management of production and the possibility of disposing of the social surplus product
to the workers as a whole—to the "associated producers."

J. N. Dawydow attempts a much more profound analysis of
the mechanisms of disalienation in the building of communism
than does Heise. To Marx—according to Dawydow—the capitalist division of labor had led to the complete elimination of
freedom from the sphere of material production; this freedom
will be restored by communism, because the needs of technique
themselves require increasing functional mobility among the producers, who will have become the principal productive force
through their scientific knowledge. The individual personality
with an all-around development becomes possible on this technical basis, which, indeed, insists upon it, since from the stand-
point of this "political economy of communism" everyone who
has not become a "fully developed individual" constitutes a serious economic loss.[23]

But this means that under increasingly general conditions of
abundance of material goods, the principal goal of production
becomes that of producing "fully" developed individuals, creative and free.[24] In proportion as man becomes the "principal productive force" [25] through the enormous extension of scientific
technology, he is less and less directly "integrated" into the production process. In proportion as "living labor" is expelled from
the production process, it acquires new significance as the organizer and controller of this process. And in proportion as there
thus take place, side by side, the production of an abundance of
material goods and the production of men with all-around development, the domination of "dead labor" over "living labor" dis-

---

22. Heise, "Uber die Entfremdung," pp. 706-707.

23. J. N. Dawydow, *Freiheit und Entfremdung* (Berlin, 1964).
p. 114.

24. Ibid., p. 117.

25. Cf. Marx, in the *Grundrisse der Kritik der politischen
Okonomie*, 2 vols. (Berlin, 1953), p. 593: "It is the development
of the social individual that [now] appears as the great fundamental pillar of production and wealth."

appears and freedom is "restored" in material production.[26]

The whole of this analysis, which is essentially based on the passages in the *Grundrisse* which I quoted earlier, seems a contribution to a fundamental clarification of the problem.[27] Its chief weakness is that it jumps in one leap from capitalist society to *communist* production relations, without analyzing the necessary and inevitable intermediate historical stages—without describing the concrete driving forces of progressive disalienation in the transitional phase, during the building of socialism. Workers' self-management, democratic-centralist central planning, the progressive withering away of commodity production, the generalization of higher education, a radical reduction in the working day, the development of creative activity during "free time," the progressive interpenetration of consumer habits on a world scale, the psychological revolution brought about by these successive transformations, and in particular by the withering away of commodity production:[28] none of this is included in Dawydow's analysis, and they are needed in order to complete it and remove from his work a touch of platitudinism which his bourgeois and dogmatist critics may wrongly use against him.[29]

The point is that, in order to be logical the analysis of the progressive disalienation of labor and of man under socialism must be combined with an exhaustive analysis of alienation in the transition period. Without this, such an analysis becomes arbitrary. It looks like a "flight into the future" which irritates those who give priority to a more pragmatic approach to immediate reality. At least, though, this "flight into the future" has the merit of clarity

---

26. Dawydow, *Freiheit und Entfremdung*, pp. 117, 131.

27. See the series of quotations given in Chapter 7 of my *The Formation of the Economic Thought of Karl Marx* (New York and London, 1971).

28. I have devoted a large part of Chapter 17 of my *Marxist Economic Theory* to these problems.

29. Several aspects of Dawydow's argument have already begun to be verified empirically, in particular the need for a greater degree of mobility of labor and the ability to perform tasks within functional teams which is resulting from the advance of automation in large-scale industry. (See G. Friedmann and P. Naville, eds., *Traité de sociologie du travail*, Vol. I, Paris, 1961, pp. 380-381).

and precision in its view of future developments. It remains faithful to Marx's teaching, which repudiates any "anthropological" conception of alienation.

The same merit cannot be accorded to the disillusioned conclusions Adam Schaff draws from his confrontation with present-day Polish reality. He recognizes that the phenomena of alienation are still to be found in socialist society, but solves the problem by casting doubt on the possibility of achieving, even in communist society, the withering away of the state, the disappearance of the division of labor (which he conceives mechanistically: a reading of Dawydow should change his view of this!), and the abolition of commodity production.[30] This skeptical and misanthropic revision of Marx has been criticized by the leaders of the Polish Communist Party[31]—not by calling for a frank analysis of the obstacles to disalienation imposed by the bureaucratized social reality of their country, but by simply denying, in the usual manner of apologetics, that the problem exists at all. Schaff, who has at least tried to draw up a "program of action" against alienation, is by comparison more sincere.[32] But both they and he are incapable of recalling what Marx taught, and therefore cannot check the rise of non-Marxist philosophy and sociology in Poland.

An example of this is the statement by sociologist Stanislaw Ossowski that the classical concept of social class formulated by Marx applies only to a type of society characterized by the capitalism of free competition. Today not only the appropriation of the means of production but also that of consumer goods permits,

---

30. "I merely mention this problem, especially because it may be supposed that commodity production will have vanished from fully developed communist society, though this supposition seems problematic [!] in the light of present-day experience." (Schaff, *Marxismus und das menschliche Individuum*, p. 177.)

31. *Nowe Drogi*, December 1965.

32. Schaff admits that the socialization of the means of production can only begin the process of disalienation. But he stresses socialist education rather than changes in economic conditions (especially the necessary withering away of bourgeois norms of distribution) as the means for completing this process. His plea for a "moderate egalitarianism" and greater freedom of opinion and of criticism in relation to "the elite in power" is to his credit, but does not go to the heart of the matter.

he says, the establishment of "economic domination over men."
There are also new forms of "domination of man by man, domination which results either from ownership of the means of production, or from ownership of the means of consumption, or from
ownership of the means of violence, or from a combination of
these different ownerships." [33] Here we plainly pass from a sociology based on the ideas of social class and social surplus product to a sociology based on the concept, infinitely vaguer and
less operative, of "dominant groups." [34] And a bridge is thus
established between critical but revisionist sociology (and philosophy) in the so-called socialist countries and the academic sociology of the capitalist countries, which rejects Marxism in favor
of a division of society into "those who command" and "those
who obey."

There is no need to underline the apologetic character of this
conception of "industrial society" as set out by various writers.
What is specific to the capitalist mode of production is attributed
to every society in the epoch of large-scale industry.[35] The results of a type of *social* organization are attributed to a form of
technical organization.

Most Western sociologists draw pessimistic conclusions from
this mystificating identification of social relations with technical
relations. They revive the old myth of Hobbes's Leviathan and
see modern man as inevitably crushed beneath the machine that
has issued from his own brain. The alienation of labor, the crush-

---

33. Stanislaw   Ossowski,   *Klassenstruktur   im   sozialen
Bewusstsein* (Berlin, 1962), pp. 227-228.

34. Ossowski's ideas are close to those of François Perroux
or Rolf Dahrendorf, quoted earlier, or to the concepts of the
conservative anthropologist Arnold Gehlen: functional authority
is said to be increasingly replacing the division of society into
classes. (*Anthropologische Forschung*, Hamburg, 1961, p. 130.)
Ossowski himself indicates (p. 223) that it is the incapacity
of the dogmatic and apologetic "Marxism" of the Stalin era
to explain the phenomena of social privilege in societies with
socialized means of production that lies at the root of his skeptical
revisionism.

35. See in particular Raymond Aron, *Dix-huit leçons sur la
société industrielle*; Reinhard Bendix, *Work and Authority in
Industry*; Dahrendorf, *Class and Class Conflict in Industrial
Society*.

ing of the worker by his own product, is said to be the inevitable result of large-scale industry, and this alienation, we are told, will relentlessly worsen as the technical apparatus is perfected.

It must be admitted that the bureaucratic degeneration of the U.S.S.R., especially in the Stalin era, has furnished plenty of arguments for supporters of this pessimistic view. But what is char-

acteristic of most of them is the absence from their writings of an analysis in depth which would bring out the *laws of development* of social reality from a purely phenomenological description of it.

By stating that there will always be "those who command" and "those who obey," that there will always be scarce goods and the necessity of an alienating method of alloting them, these authors raise to the level of an axiom not the conclusions but the premises of their argument. They think they are basing themselves on empirical facts, but in reality they are refusing to recognize a *tendency* that is going in the opposite direction. For it is hard to deny that the potential wealth of society, the degree of satisfaction of rational needs, and the possibility of thereby eliminating the coercive mechanisms in the social and economic organization, have been advancing with giant strides for a whole century—and especially in the last quarter of this century—in what is called "industrial" society. Why should it be supposed that this tendency cannot result in a qualitative "leap," by which man's enslavement to the necessities of a "struggle for existence" would wither away and his capacity to dominate his own social organization, no less than he dominates the forces of nature, would come to full flower?

It must be recognized that technical development is not heading in the direction foreseen by the pessimists. Georg Klaus correctly distinguishes between *two* types of automation, the second of which, much less rigid than the first and based on cybernetics, creates the infrastructure for the withering away of alienating labor and is the precondition for all-around creative labor. And a scientist like A. G. M. Van Melsen honestly admits that technique is still in the primitive stage, with many of its brutalizing aspects resulting precisely from this primitiveness: "When the primary needs have really been satisfied, it is perfectly possible, partly as a result of technical progress itself, to produce many small series and to incorporate original artistic projects in each of these series. Moreover, the shorter and shorter length of time needed for 'obligatory labor' helps to make possible the blossoming of all those things that demand so much personal care and love. . . . No doubt they will come back in the form of free arts practiced by those who will have been liberated by technique." [36] It goes without saying that technique cannot play this liberating role until it has been freed from the grip of private profit and the exploitation of capital.

The pronounced pessimism of the supporters of the thesis that alienation is inevitable in "industrial society" is explained by their confusing the *real sources of authority* with the *functional articulation of authority*.[37] The board of directors of a capitalist company can decide to close down its enterprises, destroying the entire bureaucratic hierarchy patiently built up, without ever having previously encroached on the "growing independence" of the research laboratories or the technological planning department. But its decision to dissolve the company, made from considerations of profit-making, shows how the previous delegation of authority was limited to particular functions and how it is that private property remains the real source of authority. Why could a workers' council not delegate some technical authority in the same way, without thereby ceasing to be able to make (or even to cause the collective groups of workers to make) the basic decisions of *economic management?*

---

36. Georg Klaus, *Kybernetik in philosophischer Sicht* (Berlin, 1965), pp. 414-415; A. G. M. Van Melsen, *Science and Technology* (Pittsburgh, 1960), p. 321.

37. Typical in this connection are the thoughts of Alain Touraine on the increasing decentralization of decisions within large "bureaucratized" enterprises, in Friedmann and Naville, eds., *Traité de sociologie du travail,* Vol. I. pp. 420 *et seq.* One of the first to use this argument was Johann Plenge the true ancestor of present-day bourgeois criticism of Marx: "Modern technique implies mental work, it implies the subordination of disciplined manual work in the enterprise as a whole," and so the exercise of power by the manual workers is impossible. (*Marx und Hegel,* p. 134.) This passage should be set beside that taken from Wolfgang Heise, above, concerning the impossibility of democracy within an enterprise owing to the "differentiation of social functions." We see that the apologia for the bourgeois hierarchy in the factory provides the main argument in the apologia for the bureaucratic hierarchy.

It is not the technical inevitability of this functional articulation that makes it impossible to "democratize the enterprises." It is not the complexity and the increasing differentiation of tasks that hinder this democratization. The insurmountable obstacle under capitalism is the ultimate right of making the final decisions which the big shareholders and their allies and representatives, the managers, want to keep for themselves.[38] Once this obstacle has been swept away by the socialist revolution there is no *a priori* reason to suppose that "fresh alienations" must arise from technical necessities within enterprises under democratic-centralist self-management.

The same pessimism also results from inadequately distinguishing between the *apparent automatism of the mechanisms* and the *human decisions inspired by social and economic motives* which are characteristic of what is called "industrial" society. When writers like Norbert Wiener fear that machines will eventually make decisions independently of any judgment by men (themselves mechanized),[39] they forget that in capitalist society the tendency to mechanize labor at the lower levels is accompanied by an unprecedented concentration of *power to decide* at the top, where a handful of men—aided by an enormous mass of information and relying on the entire functional articulation of authority which immensely strengthens its striking power—remain the sole masters who, in the final instance, decide whether a particular line of action *suggested* by the computers will actually be adopted or not.[40] What Marxist theory illuminates is

---

38. François Bloch-Laîné brings this out strikingly in *Pour une réforme de l'enterprise* (Paris, 1963), pp. 41, 43-44, 100: He argues for greater participation by the trade unions and the workers in the management of *certain* aspects of the activity of the enterprises. But he immediately emphasizes that this "participation" leaves untouched the single supreme authority, the master hierarchy which alone retains the right to make the key economic decisions.

39. Norbert Wiener, *The Human Use of Human Beings* (New York, 1954), pp. 158-160.

40. The case of the American war machine, which is highly mechanized (especially as regards the warning system, guided by computers), but which culminates in the President of the United States, who alone has the right to press certain buttons,

the *motives* that ultimately inspire these men: not arbitrary motives, or irrational ones, or mere speculation, but the overall defense of class interests as these are understood by the most powerful stratum of the class concerned.

If, then, this is how matters really stand, it is clear that it is enough to transfer this power of decision from a small handful of men to the mass of "associated producers" for these same machines to be made to *serve* society to the same extent that today they seem to *enslave* it.[41]

Alongside these pessimistic mystifications, however, there are also some optimistic ones. The alienation of labor, it is said, is indeed an inevitable result of "industrial society," but it can be overcome without the necessity of overthrowing capitalism. It will be enough to give back to the workers a "sense of participation," or even a "work ethic"—thanks to human relations being given back their value within the enterprise—for the workers no longer to feel alienated.[42] It will be necessary, say others, to insure the existence of means of communication, dialogue, and creation which give back to the worker his sense of personality and his freedom in work and leisure.[43]

The first of these theses is plainly apologetic in character. I will even say that it undoubtedly serves big capital in a direct way, since its avowed aim is to reduce social conflicts *under the existing regime*. What the specialists in "human relations" try to abolish is not the reality of alienation but the workers' awareness of this reality. Their pseudo-disalienation would be alienation carried to an extreme, with the alienated worker alienated from

is symbolic of the entire mechanism of the capitalist regime.

41. Here is a striking example of the confusion between the *socioeconomic power of decision* and technical authority, taken from the German bourgeois newspaper *Frankfurter Allgemeine Zeitung* of August 16, 1967. A writer argues that with all the demands for self-management we hear nowadays, why not demand that a "patients' council" have the right to dictate to doctors about diagnoses and treatments?

42. Elton Mayo, *The Human Problems of an Industrial Civilization* (New York, 1960), pp. 158-159, 171 *et seq.*; Bendix, *Work and Authority in Industry* (New York, 1956), pp. 448-450.

43. François Perroux, "Aliénation et création collective," in *Cahiers de l'ISEA,* June 1964, pp. 92-93.

awareness of his own condition as a mutilated human being.[44]

Alienation thus acquires additional dimensions through the attempt made by bourgeois society to manipulate not merely the thinking and the habits but even the unconscious of the producers.[45] There is little chance, however, that the technicians of "human relations" will in the long run be able to prevent the workers from becoming aware of the state of oppression in which they find themselves.

The second thesis, a more subtle one, is above all ambiguous. It is formulated as a moral imperative, apparently independent of the "form taken by institutions" (that is, the mode of production). But François Perroux explains that "it is not within a rigid framework of institutions, consecrating the wrong and injustice in society as a whole, that specialized institutions can fulfill their function." [46] Is a society based on the *obligation* of the worker to sell his labor power and to carry on brutalizing work in order to obtain the means to live not a "rigid framework consecrating wrong and injustice"? How can one give the worker, within that framework, "the feeling that he is participating in collective

---

44. Bendix correctly classifies the theory of "human relations" in the larger category of "ideology of management" (I should call it, rather, capitalist ideology concerning the enterprise). It would be easy to show that the evolution of this ideology, over a century, reflects not only the evolution of the structure of the capitalist enterprise itself but also and above all the evolution of the balance of strength between bourgeoisie and proletariat. Nothing is more revealing in this connection than the change from the haughty Puritanism and social Darwinism of the age when the capitalist was all-powerful to the hypocritical pleas for association between capital and labor which nowadays abound.

45. Vance Packard, *The Hidden Persuaders*. While C. Wright Mills fears the development of indifference in the face of alienation (*The Marxists*, p. 113), Bloch-Laîné stresses, more realistically, with regard to this same alienation or at least its most striking aspect (the absence of workers' power within the enterprises): "The calm is deceptive. Behind it lie many special and individual dissatisfactions, which are ready to break out into revolt at the first downward turn of the general economic situation." (*Pour une réforme de l'entreprise*, p. 25.) See some bibliographical references on the state of mind of the working class in Chapter 1.

46. "Aliénation et création collective," p. 44.

creation," or "the opportunity and the means to become conscious of himself" during his leisure hours? Under the capitalist mode of production this would be nothing but a crude deception. Carrying out this program requires overthrowing capitalist society. From that moment onward, however, Perroux's program would undergo a remarkable expansion. It would no longer be a question of giving the worker the "feeling" of participating in collective creation, but of making him a real creator. It would no longer be a matter of giving him the opportunity and the means to "become conscious of himself" in his leisure hours, but of giving him the opportunity to realize himself through free creation, without external constraint. It would no longer be a matter of allowing "beneficent zones" of "disinterested curiosity" to develop, but of attaining complete self-management by men in all spheres of social activity.

For that is where the key to ultimate disalienation really lies. It results from the abolition of labor (in the sense in which Marx and Engels mean this in *The German Ideology*),[47] or, in other words, the replacement of mechanical and schematic labor by really creative labor which is no longer labor in the traditional sense of the word, which no longer leads to a man's giving up his life in order to insure his material existence, but has become man's all-around creative activity.[48]

---

47. *The German Ideology* (Moscow, 1964), pp. 85, 95, 236, 242.

48. Cf. Georg Klaus: "In order to develop all man's creative powers, it is necessary to free him to a large extent from the obligation to contribute schematic labor . . . " "Cybernetics and automation are the technical conditions for this situation [communism], because they enable man to free himself from all noncreative, schematic work . . . They give him above all the time for an all-around scientific and technical education, that is, for truly creative labor at the contemporary level of production." (*Kybernetik in philosophischer Sicht*, pp. 457, 464.)

The Problem of Alienation

by George Novack

The international socialist movement is witnessing a crusade in its own ranks nowadays for Moral Rearmament. To support their conclusions the intellectual apostles of this new tendency lean heavily upon the alienations suffered by man in modern society. Mixing socialist doctrines with psychoanalytical theory, they approach the the problem of alienation as though it were pivotal in modern life and treat it as though it were the very center of Marxist thought.

Their preoccupation with the question has been stimulated by numerous commentaries on recent translations of such early writings of Marx and Engels as *The Economic and Philosophic Manuscripts of 1844, The Holy Family* and *The German Ideology* in which the concept of alienation plays a large part.

The intensified interest in this subject is not a mere crotchet of the radical intellectuals. It stems from the very real alienations experienced in present-day society and from the growing antagonism between the rulers and the ruled in both the capitalist and post-capitalist sectors of the world.

The contradictions of life under contemporary capitalism engender deep-going feelings of frustration. The wealth pouring from the factories and the farms during the prolonged postwar boom has not strengthened assurance about the future. Instead, it has become another source

of anxiety, for it is widely felt that a new depression will
follow. Similarly, the enhanced control over industrial
processes made possible by automation confronts the
workers, not with welcome release from burdensome toil,
but with the specter of chronic unemployment. The command over nature involved in the tapping of nuclear
energy holds over humanity's head the threat of total
annihilation rather than the promise of peace and plenty.
An uncontrolled inner circle of capitalist politicians and
military leaders decide matters of life and death. No wonder that people feel the economic and political forces
governing their fate as alien powers.

Although the social soil is different, similar sentiments
are widely spread in the post-capitalist countries dominated
by the bureaucratic caste. Despite the great advances in
science, technology, industry, public health and other fields
made possible by their revolutions, workers and peasants,
students and intellectuals keenly resent their lack of control
over the government and the administration of the
economy. Freedom of thought, expression and organization are denied them. Despite the official propaganda
that they have at least become masters of their own des-
tinies, the people know that the powers of decision in the
most vital affairs are exercised, not by them, but by bureaucratic caliphs. The cardinal duty of the masses in the
Communist Party, the unions, the factories and collective
farms, the educational institutions and publishing houses
is still to obey the dictates from above.

That now discarded handbook of falsifications of history
and Marxism edited by Stalin, *The History of the Communist Party of the Soviet Union*, closes with the admonition
that the "Bolsheviks" will be strong and invincible only
so long as "they maintain connection with their mother,
the masses, who gave birth to them, suckled them and
reared them." Krushchev has told how Stalin in his later
years never visited the factories or farms and was totally
insulated from the lives of ordinary folk. But Stalin's
successor has lifted only a corner of the veil hiding the
profound estrangement of the Soviet masses from the
"boss men," as they are called.

Many thoughtful members of the Communist Party have

been impelled by the revelations at the Twentieth Congress
of the CPSU and by the Polish and Hungarian events of
1956 to reconsider their former views. Some of them seek
an explanation for the crimes of the Soviet leaders and the
Stalinist perversions of socialism in the Marxist oulook
itself.

This search has led them back to the young Marx.
They believe that they have found in the early works,
which mark his transition from Hegelianism through Humanism to dialectical materialism, the clue to the falsifications of Marxism and the distortions of socialism which
have run rampant in the Soviet Union and the Communist
parties. In these observations of Marx on the alienation
of mankind under class society, in particular, they see
the basis for a salutary regeneration of the tarnished
socialist ideal.

These intellectuals have raised the banner of a neo-
Socialist Humanism against "mechanical materialism" and
"economic automatism." The seeds of the evil that bore
such bitter fruits under Stalin, they claim, were planted by
the "mechanical" Marxists and cultivated by the crudely
materialistic Leninists. They call for a renovated morality
and a more sensitive concern for the "concrete, whole,
living man." Monstrous forms of totalitarianism are produced by subservience to such "abstractions" as the Forces
of Production, the Economic Foundations and the Cultural
Superstructure, they say. Such an immoral and inhuman
materialism leads to the reappearance, behind socialist
phrases, of the rule of things over people imposed by
capitalism.

The same message was proclaimed over two decades
ago in the United States by Dwight MacDonald, then
editor of *Politics*, and by the Johnson-Forest group in the
Socialist Workers Party. It is a favorite theme of the Social
Democratic and ex-Trotskyist writers of the magazine
Dissent. It is now becoming the creed of some former
Communist Party intellectuals grouped around *The New
Reasoner* in England.

E. P. Thompson, one of the two editors of *The New
Reasoner,* wrote in a programmatic pronouncement in the
first issue (summer, 1957): "The ideologies of capitalism

and Stalinism are both forms of 'self-alienation'; men stumble in their minds and lose themselves in abstractions; capitalism sees human labor as a commodity and the satisfaction of his 'needs' as the production and distribution of commodities; Stalinism sees labor as an economic-physical act in satisfying economic-physical needs. Socialist humanism declares: liberate men from slavery to things, to the pursuit of profit or servitude to 'economic necessity.' Liberate man, as a creative being—and he will create, not only new values, but things in scope and abundance."

Despite their up-to-date reasoning, the "new thoughts" brought forward by such Socialist Humanists against dialectical materialism are hardly original. The essence of their viewpoint is to be found in the schools of petty-bourgeois socialism which flourished in Germany before the Revolution of 1848. Scientific socialism was created in struggle against these doctrines, as anyone familiar with the ideological birth process of Marxism knows.

The "True Socialism" of Moses Hess and Karl Grun sought to base the socialist movement, not upon the necessary historical development of economic conditions and the struggles of class forces, but upon abstract principles and ethical precepts regarding the need for mankind, divided against itself, to recover its wholeness and universality. In the section on "True Socialism" in *The Communist Manifesto* Marx and Engels ridiculed these phrasemongers who talked about the "alienation of the essence of mankind" instead of undertaking a scientific investigation of money and its functions.

In their justified revulsion from Stalinism, the new "humane" socialists have not gone forward to genuine Marxism, as they mistakenly believe; they have landed behind it. They have unwittingly relapsed into a stage of theoretical development that socialism and its materialist philosophy surmounted over a century ago. What is worse, in taking this backward leap to a prescientific socialism of the most mawkish variety, they discard both the materialist principles and the dialectical method which constitute the heart of Marxism.

The attempts of these disoriented intellectuals to insert abstract moralistic foundations under Marxism are retro-

gressive. Yet it must be admitted that the theory of alienation is by no means foreign to Marxism. It did play an
influential part in the genesis and formative period of
scientific socialism. Indeed, in the history of the concept
we find a striking example of how the founders of Marxism
divested Hegel's central conceptions of their "idealist
trappings" and placed them on solid materialist supports,
transforming both their form and substance in the process.
It is worthwhile to ascertain what the Marxist attitude
toward alienation really is. This will be the best corrective
to the wanderings of those upset socialists who are
fumbling for a new equilibrium.

Marx took the concept of alienation from Hegel. In this
instance, as in so many others, Hegelianism was the
ideological source and starting point of Marxian thought.

Alienation (*Entausserung*) and estrangement (*Entfremdung*) are key categories in Hegel's idealist philosophy.
These are the most extreme expressions of difference or
"otherness." In the process of change everything necessarily
has a divided and antithetical nature, for it is both itself
and, at the same time, becoming something else, its "other."
But viewed as a whole, the "other" is simply a development of the "itself"; the implicit becomes explicit; the possible
actual. This process is a dual one. It involves *estrangement* from the original form and the *realization* of the
essence in a higher form of existence.

In his system Hegel applied this dialectical logic to the
evolution of the "Absolute," his synonym for the whole
of reality. The Absolute first exists as mere Logical Idea,
self-enclosed like a bud. It breaks out of itself by way of
an inner revolution (just how and why is not clear) to a
completely alienated condition — Nature. Hegel saw Nature
as a lifeless dispersed mode of existence in contradiction
to the lively perpetual movement and universal intercon-
nection inherent in the Absolute.

This contradiction drives the Idea forward through a
prolonged course of development until it emerges from
its material casing and appears as Mind. Mind in turn
passes through a series of stages from crude sensation
to its highest peak in philosophy, and above all in Hegel's
own idealist outlook.

Throughout this complex process alienation plays the most positive role. It is the expression of the Negative at work. The Negative, forever destroying existing forms through the conflict of opposites, spurs everything onward to a higher mode of existence. For Hegel a specific kind of alienation may be historically necessary at one stage, even though it is cancelled out at the next in the universal interplay of the dialectic.

All of this may appear to be a dull chapter in the life of the German universities of a century and a half ago. But Hegel saw the development of society as one of the outcomes of this evolution of the Idea. Moreover, he traced the course of alienation in human history. He noted such curious items as the fact that humans alone of all the creatures on earth can take the objective conditions around them and transform them into a medium of humanity's subjective development. Despite the bizarreness of considering a material process like that to be an expression of the evolution of Idea, such observations, it will be recognized, have a modern ring.

Still more, at turning points in their development, Hegel pointed out, humans find themselves in deep conflict with the world around them. Their own material and spiritual creations have risen up and passed beyond their control. Ironically humans become enslaved to their own productions. All this the great philosopher saw with astounding clarity.

Hegel applied the notion of the alienation of humanity from itself to the transitional period between the fall of the Greek city-states and the coming of Christianity; and above all to the bourgeois society around him. Early in his career he described industrial society as "a vast system of mutual interdependence, *a moving life of the dead.* This system moves hither and yon in a blind elementary way, and like a wild animal calls for strong permanent control and curbing." (*Jenenser Realphilosophie*, p. 237) He looked to the state to impose that control over capitalist competition.

Of still livelier interest to our nuclear age, he had some sharp things to say about the institution of private property which forces people to live in a world that, although their creation, is opposed to their deepest needs. This "dead" world, foreign to human nature, is governed by inexorable laws which oppress humanity and rob it of freedom.

Hegel also emphasized that the complete subordination of the individual to the division of labor in commodity-producing society cripples and represses human development. Mechanization, the very means which should liberate man from toil, makes him still more a slave.

On the political plane, especially in his earlier writings, Hegel discussed how, in the Germany of his day, the individual was estranged from the autocratic state because he could not participate in its affairs.

The very need for philosophy itself, according to Hegel, springs from these all-embracing contradictions in which human existence has been plunged. The conflict of society against nature, of idea against reality, of consciousness against existence, Hegel generalizes into the conflict between "subject" and "object." This opposition arises from the alienation of Mind from itself. The world of objects, originally the product of Man's labor and knowledge, becomes independent and opposed to man. The objective world becomes dominated by uncontrollable forces and overriding laws in which man can no longer recognize or realize his true self. At the same time, and as a result of the same process, thought becomes estranged from reality. The truth becomes an impotent ideal preserved in thought alone while the actual world functions apart from its influence.

This brings about an "unhappy consciousness" in which man is doomed to frustration unless he succeeds in reuniting the severed parts of his world. Nature and society have to be brought under the sway of man's reason so that the sundered elements of his essential self can be reintegrated. How is this opposition between an irrational world and an ineffectual reason to be overcome? In other words, how can the world be made subject to reason and reason itself become effective?

Philosophy in such a period of general disintegration, Hegel declared, can discover and make known the principle and method to bring about the unity mankind needs.

Reason (we almost wrote *The New Reasoner*) is the au-
thentic form of reality in which the antagonisms of subject
and object are eliminated, or rather transmuted into the
genuine unity and universality of mankind.

Hegel related the opposition of subject and object to
concrete antagonisms. In his own philosophical language
he was struggling to express the consequences of capitalist
conditions where people are misled by a false and distorted
consciousness of their real relations with one another
and where they cannot make their wills effective because
they are overwhelmed by the unmanageable laws of the
market.

Hegel further maintained that the solution of such contradictions was a matter of practice as well as of philosophic theory. Inspired by the French Revolution, he
envisaged the need for a similar "reign of reason" in his
own country. But he remained a bourgeois thinker who
never transcended his idealist philosophy in viewing the
relations of class society. In his most progressive period
Hegel did not offer any practical recommendations for
overcoming existing social antagonisms that went beyond
the bounds of bourgeois reform.

It was only through the subsequent work of Marx that
these idealistic reflections of an irrational social reality
were placed in their true light. Against Hegel's interpreta-
tion of alienation, Marx showed what the historical origins,
material basis and real nature of this phenomenon were.

Marx began his intellectual life as an ardent Hegelian.
Between 1843 and 1848, under the influence of Feuerbach,
he cleared his mind of what he later called "the old junk"
and emerged together with Engels as a full-fledged materialist.

The "humane" socialists are now embarked on the
quixotic venture of reversing this progressive sequence.
They aim to displace the mature Marx, the thoroughgoing
dialectical materialist, with the youthful Marx who had
yet to pass beyond the one-sided materialism of Feuerbach.

Marx recognized that the concept of alienation reflected
extremely significant aspects of social life. He also became
aware that Hegel's idealism and Feuerbach's abstract
Humanism obscured the real historical conditions and

social contradictions that had generated the forms of alienation.

Marx did not reach his ripest conclusions on this subject all at once but only by successive approximations over decades of scientific study. Between his Hegelian starting point and his final positions there was an interim period of discovery, during which he developed his preliminary conclusions.

Marx first undertook the study of political economy, which occupied the rest of his life, in 1843. He pursued this task along with a criticism of his Hegelian heritage. The first results were set down in the *Economic and Philosophic Manuscripts* he wrote primarily for his own clarification during 1844. These were published posthumously in our own time and did not appear in their first complete English translation until 1959.*

These essays were Marx's earliest attempt at analyzing capitalism. In them for the first time he applied the dialectical method learned from Hegel to the categories of political economy. In many passages his ideas are formulated so abstractly and abstrusely that it is not easy to decipher their meaning without a grasp of the terminology and mode of thought prevalent in German classical philosophy.

Whereas in his later works (*The Critique of Political Economy, Capital*) Marx takes the commodity as the cell of capitalism, he here puts forward alienated labor as the central concept. He even views private property as derived from the alienation of labor. It is both the product of estranged labor, he writes, and the means by which labor is estranged from itself. "Just as we have derived the concept of private property from the concept of estranged alienated labor by analysis, in the same way every category of political economy can be evolved with the help of these two factors; and we shall find again in each category, for example, trade, competition, capital, money, only a definite and developed expression of these first foundations," he declares.

---

*See *Economic and Philosophic Manuscripts of* 1844 by Karl Marx, published by the Foreign Languages Publishing House, Moscow.

Having established alienated labor as the basis and beginning of capitalist production, Marx then deduces the consequences. Labor becomes alienated when the producer works, not directly for himself or a collective united by common interests, but for another with interests and aims opposed to his own.

This antagonistic relation of production injures the worker in many ways. (1) He is estranged from his own body which must be maintained as a physical subject, not because it is part of himself, but so that it can function as an element of the productive process. (2) He is estranged from nature since natural objects with all their variety function, not as means for his self-satisfaction or cultural fulfillment, but merely as material means for profitable production. (3) He is estranged from his own peculiar essence as a human being because his special traits and abilities are not needed, used or developed by his economic activities which degrade him to the level of a mere physical force. (4) Finally, he is separated from his fellow human beings. "Where man is opposed to himself, he also stands opposed to other men."

Consequently the dispossessed worker benefits neither from the activity of his labor nor from its product. These do not serve as means for his enjoyment or fulfillment as an individual because both are appropriated by someone other than himself, the capitalist. "If the worker's activity is torment to himself, it must be the enjoyment and satisfaction of another."

The object which labor creates, the labor product, becomes opposed to man as an alien essence, as a power independent of the producer. "Wage-labor, like private property, is only a necessary consequence of the alienation of labor." Society can be emancipated from both private property and servitude only by abolishing wage-labor.

Marx honored Hegel for seeing that man is the result of his conditions of labor. He found this primary proposition of historical materialism in Hegel, though in an idealist shape. The greatness of the *Phenomenology*, Marx observed, lies in the circumstance that "Hegel conceives the self-production of man as a process . . ."

Marx criticizes Hegel for seeing only one side of this

process, the alienation of consciousness, and neglecting the most important aspect of labor in class society, the alienation of the actual man who produces commodities. Marx accepted Feuerbach's view that Hegel's philosophy was itself an abstract expression of the alienation of mankind from itself. Hegel's Absolute Idealism separated the thought process from real active thinking persons and converted it into an independent, all-powerful subject which absorbed the world into itself. At bottom, it was a sophisticated form of religious ideology in which the Logical Idea replaced God.

In the Hegelian dialectic, Nature, the antithesis to the Idea, was nothing in and for itself; it was merely a concealed and mysterious embodiment of the Absolute Idea. However, Marx, following Feuerbach, pointed out that this Absolute Idea was itself nothing but "a thing of thought," a generalized expression for the thinking process of real individuals dependent on nature.

Marx pays tribute to Feuerbach for exposing the religious essence of Hegel's system and thereby reestablishing the materialist truth that Nature, instead of being an expression of the Idea, is the real basis for thought and the ultimate source of all ideas.

Hegel, Marx said, discovered "the abstract, logical and speculative expression for the movement of history." What Marx sought to do was to uncover the real motive forces in history (comprising both nature and society in their development, as he was to emphasize in *The German Ideology*) which preceded all theorizing and provided both the materials and the motives for the operations of thought.

Moreover, Hegel had mistakenly identified all externalization of man's vital powers in nature and society with alienation because it represented an inferior grade of the Idea's existence. Actually, the objectification of his capacities is normal and necessary to the human being and is the mainspring of all progress. It is perverted into alienation only under certain historical conditions which are not eternal.

Many brilliant thoughts are to be found in the pages of *The Economic and Philosophic Manuscripts*. For example, Marx brings out the differences between the animal and human senses in a way that counterposes his historical materialism to vulgar materialism. Sensation is the basis for human knowledge as well as for the materialist theory of knowledge. Although the human sensory equipment is animal in origin, it develops beyond that. Human senses pass through an historical, social and cultural development which endow us with far more discriminating modes of sensation than any known in the animal state. "The cultivation of the five senses is the work of the whole history of the world to date," he concludes.

Capitalism is to be condemned because it blunts sensitivity instead of sharpening it. The dealer in gems who sees only their market value, and not the beauty and unique character of minerals, "has no mineralogical sensitivity," he writes; he is little different from an animal grubbing for food. The task of civilization is to develop a specifically human sensitivity "for the whole wealth of human and natural essence."

An entire school of contemporary American sociologists, headed by David Reisman, has based its analysis of the condition of men in "the mass society" on the fact that the average person is bored and depressed by the drudgery of his work in factory or office and finds satisfaction for his individual needs only in leisure hours. The split between labor and leisure under capitalism was long ago noted by Marx in these manuscripts where he pointed out: "Labor is external to the worker, i. e., it does not belong to his essential being. Therefore he does not affirm himself in his work but denies himself. He does not feel contented but dissatisfied. He does not develop freely his physical and spiritual energy but mortifies his body and ruins his mind. The worker therefore only feels himself to be himself outside his work, and in his work he feels outside himself. He is at home when he is not working, and when he is working, he is not at home."

Marx did not leave the concept of labor as treated in these early essays. Extending the range of his criticism of bourgeois political economy and probing deeper into the secrets of capitalist production, he filled out and corrected his original presentation. He developed the features and forms of labor into a brilliant constellation of diversified determinations, reflecting the facets of the many-sided relations of production in their historical evolution.

The younger Marx, swayed by Feuerbach's Humanism, analyzed capitalist relations by counterposing what is dehumanized to what is truly human. The later Marx viewed them in terms of class oppositions.

Most important was his discovery of the twofold character of labor: the concrete labor which produces use-values and the abstract labor which produces exchange value. In abstract labor Marx found the essence of alienated labor in commodity-producing societies. His discovery, which Engels rightly lauded as Marx's chief contribution to the science of political economy, enabled him to explain the nature of commodities and the source of value as well as such mysteries as the power of money. The distinction between the two kinds of labor asserts itself at every decisive point in his analysis.

Marx took another step beyond his predecessors by distinguishing between labor as a concrete activity which creates specific use-values and labor power, the value-producing property of labor. He demonstrated how the peculiar characteristics of labor power as a commodity make capitalist exploitation possible. He also showed that the exploitation of labor in general, under all modes of class production, is based on the difference between necessary and surplus labor.

It would require a summary of the whole of *Capital* to deal with all of Marx's amplifications of the concept of labor. The pertinent point is this: the complex relations between capital and labor which were sketched in broad outline in the early essays were developed into a network of precise distinctions. The concept of alienated labor was broken down into elements integrated into a comprehensive exposition of the laws of motion of capitalism.

Before examining the specific causes of alienation under capitalism, it is necessary to note that the phenomenon is rooted in the whole previous history of humanity. The process by which man becomes oppressed by his own creations has passed through distinct stages of evolution.

The most primitive forms of alienation arise from the disparity between man's needs and wishes and his control over nature. Although they have grown strong enough to counterpose themselves as a collective laboring body against the natural environment, primitive peoples do not have enough productive forces, techniques and knowledge to assert much mastery over the world around them. Their helplessness in material production has its counterpart in the power of magic and religion in their social life and thought. Religion, as Feuerbach explained and Marx repeated, reverses the real relations between mankind and the world. Man created the gods in his own image. But to the superstitious mind, unaware of unconscious mental processes, it appears that the gods have created men. Deluded by such appearances — and by social manipulators from witch doctors to priests — men prostrate themselves before idols of their own manufacture. The distance between the gods and the mass of worshippers serves as a gauge for estimating the extent of man's alienation from his fellow men and his subjugation to the natural environment.

Alienation is therefore first of all a social expression of the fact that men lack adequate control over the forces of nature and have thereby not yet acquired control over sources of daily sustenance.

Alienation has been a general feature of human history. The *alienation of labor,* however, is peculiar to civilization and is bound up with the institution of private property. In primitive society men are oppressed by nature but not by the products of their labor.

The rudimentary alienation observable in the magic and religion found in savagery and barbarism becomes overlaid and subsequently overwhelmed by another and higher types of alienation engendered by the conditions of class society. With the development of agriculture, stock breeding and craftsmanship, the most advanced sectors of mankind became less directly dependent upon raw nature for their food supplies. They increased their sources of wealth and reduced nature's oppression.

But civilized man's growing control over nature was attended by a loss of control over the basic conditions of his economic activity. So long as production remained simple but collective, as in primitive tribal life, the producers had control over their process of production and the disposition of their product. With the extension of the social division of labor, more and more goods became converted into commodities and entered exchange in the market.

The producers thereby lost control over their product as it became subject to the laws of the commodity market. In turn, these laws came to rule the producers to such an extent that in time men themselves became commodities to be bought and sold. *Slavery was the first organized system of alienated labor; wage labor will be the last.*

Wage labor is a special type of alienated labor. In this mode of production the laborer becomes the victim of the world market, a slave to the law of supply and demand, to such a degree that he can stand idle and his dependents starve when there is no demand for his labor power as a commodity.

The historical groundwork for the alienation suffered by the working class is private property in the means of production. This enables the owners to appropriate the surplus product of the laborers. There is nothing mysterious about the material origin of alienation in class society. It comes about as a consequence of the separation of the producers from the conditions of production and thereby from what they produce. When the laborers lose control of the material means of production, they forfeit control over their lives, their liberties and their means of development.

Hegel pointed this out when he wrote in the *Philosophy of Right:* "By alienating the whole of my time, as crystalized in my work, and everything I produced, I would be making another's property the substance of my being, my universal activity and actuality, my personality."

This second kind of alienation reaches its apex under capitalism, where every individual involved in the network of production and exchange is ruled by the laws of the world market. These function as coercive external powers over which even the masters of capital have no control, as the fluctuations of the business cycle demonstrate.

The influence of the earlier type of alienation, on the other hand, based upon lack of command over the forces of nature, lessens as technology and science expand with the growth of the productive forces from one stage of civilization to the next. As Marx wrote: "The miracles of God become superfluous because of the miracles of industry." Today, when man's conquest of nature is conclusive, though far from completed, the influence of unconquered nature as a factor in producing alienation is small compared to its economic causes.

The alierations imposed by capital upon labor reinforce and intensify those forms of alienation carried over from the barbarous past by adding to them estrangements bred by capitalism's own peculiar type of exploitation. It is necessary to analyze the economic foundations of capitalist society in order to bring out its characteristic processes of alienation.

(1) Capitalism emerges as a distinct and separate economic formation by wrenching away working people from precapitalist conditions of production. Before capitalism could be established, the mass of direct producers had to be separated from the material means of production and transformed into propertyless proletarians. The processes of expropriation whereby the peasants were uprooted from the land and the social elements fashioned for the wage labor required for capitalist exploitation in Western Europe were summarized by Marx in Chapter XIX of *Capital*.

(2) However, the alienation of the producers only begins with the primary accumulation of capital; it is continually reproduced on an ever-extended scale once capital takes over industry. Even before he physically engages in the productive process, the wage-worker finds his labor taken away from him by the stipulations of the labor contract. The worker agrees to hand over his labor power to the capitalist in return for the payment of the prevailing wage. The employer is then free to use and exploit this labor as he pleases.

(3) During the productive process, by virtue of the peculiar divisions of labor in capitalist enterprise, all the knowledge, will and direction is concentrated in the cap-

italist and his superintendents. The worker is converted into a mere physical accessory factor of production. "The capitalist represents the unity and will of the social working body" while the workers who make up that body are "dehumanized" and degraded to the status of things. The plan, the process, and the aim of capitalist production all confront the workers as alien, hostile, dominating powers. The auto workers on the assembly line can testify to the truth of this fact.

(4) At the end of the industrial process the product which is its result does not belong to the workers who made it but to the capitalist who owns it. In this way the product of labor is torn from the workers and goes into the market to be sold.

(5) The capitalist market, which is the totality of commodities and money in their circulation, likewise confronts the working class — whether as sellers of their labor power or as buyers of commodities — as an alien power. Its laws of operation dictate how much they shall get for their labor power, whether it is saleable at all, what their living standards shall be.

The world market is the ultimate arbiter of capitalist society. It not only rules over the wage-slaves; it is greater than the most powerful group of capitalists. The overriding laws of the market dominate all classes like uncontrollable forces of nature which bring weal or woe regardless of anyone's plans or intentions.

(6) In addition to the fundamental antagonism between the exploiters and the exploited, the competition characteristic of capitalism's economic activities pits the members of both classes against one another. The capitalists strive to get the better of their rivals so that the bigger and more efficient devour the smaller and less productive.

The workers who go into the labor market to sell their labor power are compelled to buck one another for available jobs. In the shop and factory they are often obliged to compete against one another under the goad of piecework.

Both capitalists and workers try to mitigate the consequences of their competition by combination. The capitalists set up trusts and monopolies; the workers orga-

nize into trade unions. But however much these opposing
forms of class organization modify and restrict competition, they cannot abolish it. The competitiveness eliminated from a monopolized industry springs up more vio-
lently in the struggles between one aggregation of capital
and another. The workers in one craft, category or country
are pitted, contrary to their will, against the workers of
another.

These economic circumstances generate unbridled individualism, egotism, and self-seeking throughout bourgeois
society. The members of this society, whatever their status,
have to live in an atmosphere of mutual hostility rather
than of solidarity.

Thus the real basis of the forms of alienation within
capitalist society is found in the contradictory relations
of its mode of production and in the class antagonisms
arising from them.

Alienation, like all relations, is a two-sided affair and
its operation has contradictory consequences. What is taken
from the dispossessed is vested in the dispossessors. In
religion the feebleness of men on earth is complemented
by the omnipotence of the deity who is endowed with all
the capacities real people lack. His representatives in society, from the shamans to the clergy, exploit this situation to their advantage.

In economics, the servitude of the laborer is the basis of
the freedom of the master; the poverty of the many makes
the wealth of the few. In politics, the absence of popular
self-rule is made manifest in the despotism of the state.

In *The Economic and Philosophic Manuscripts of 1844*
Marx came to grips for the first time with the mysteries
of money. In capitalist society, he remarks, money has
displaced religion as the major source of alienation, just
as it has displaced the deity as the major object of adora-
tion and attraction. The money form of wealth stands
like a whimsical tyrant between the needs of men and
their fulfillment. The possessor of money can satisfy the
most exorbitant desires while the penniless individual cannot take care of the most elementary needs of food, clothing and shelter.

Money has the magical power of turning things into
their opposites. "Gold! Yellow, glittering, precious gold,"

can, as Shakespeare said, "make black, white; foul, fair; wrong, right; base, noble; old, young; coward, valiant." The person without artistic taste can buy and hang pictures in his mansion, or put them in a safety vault, while the creator and the genuine appreciator cannot view or enjoy them. The meanest scoundrel can purchase admiration from sycophants while worthy individuals go scorned and unnoticed.

Under capitalism, where everything enters the field of exchange and becomes the object of buying and selling, a man's worth comes to be estimated, not by his really praiseworthy abilities or actions, but by his bank account. A man is "worth" what he owns and a millionaire is "worth" incomparably more than a pauper. A Rothschild is esteemed where a Marx is hated. In this cesspool of universal venality all genuine human values and standards are distorted and desecrated.

Later, in the first chapter of *Capital*, Marx unveiled the secrets of these magical powers of money by tracing them to the forms of value acquired by the commodity in the course of its evolution. The fetishistic character of money is derived from the fetishistic character of the commodity form of value which expresses the relations between independent producers through the medium of things. The fetish of capital which commands men's lives and labor is the ultimate expression of this fetishism of commodities.

If money in the form of capital is the supreme fetish of bourgeois society, the state which enforces the economic conditions of capitalist exploitation comes a close second. State compulsion is most harshly manifested in its penal powers, its tax powers, and in its power to conscript for military service. The identity of the ordinary citizen has to be validated by documents stamped by government officials. He needs a certificate to vouch for his birth and to prove that he graduated from school; that he is married or divorced; that he may travel to other countries.

The tyranny of money and the state over the lives of people is reducible in the last analysis to the relative poverty of the social order.

The alienations embedded in the economic foundations

of capitalism manifest themselves in myriad ways in other parts of the social structure. They are crystallized in the opposition between the state and the members of society. The unity of U. S. capitalism, for example, is embodied in a state organization which is dominated and directed by representatives of the ruling monopolists.

The alienation of this government from the people in our dollar democracy is the main theme of a study of the rulers and the ruled in the United States made by Professor C. Wright Mills in *The Power Elite.* Its opening paragraph reads: "The powers of ordinary men are circumscribed by the everyday worlds in which they live, yet even in these rounds of job, family and neighborhood, they often seem driven by forces they can neither understand nor govern. 'Great changes' are beyond their control, but affect their conduct and outlook none the less. The very framework of modern society confines them to projects not their own, but from every side, such changes now press upon the men and women of the mass society, who accordingly feel that they are without purpose in an epoch in which they are without power."

Mills summed up the extreme polarization of power in our society by declaring that the big business men, statesmen and brass hats composing the power elite appear to the impotent mass as "all that we are not." To be sure, even in the mid-1950s, the population was not so stultified and inert as Mills and his fellow academic sociologists made out. The Black struggle for equality and the periodic strikes among the industrial workers indicated that much was stirring below the surface.

But it cannot be denied that the power of labor is largely untapped, unorganized, and so misdirected that its potential remains hidden even from its possessors. The policies of the union leaders help the spokesmen for "the power elite" to keep the people from envisioning the immense political strength they could wield for their own cause. They thereby keep the working class alienated from its rightful place in American political life as leader and organizer of the whole nation. This role is handed over by default to the capitalist parties.

However, the dispossession of the working class from

its historical functions will not be maintained forever. Sooner or later, the labor movement will be obliged to tear loose from its subordination to alien class political organizations and form its independent political party. This will be the beginning of a process of political self-realization, an ascent to the position of supremacy now held by the capitalist minority. If today the plutocracy is, to the masses, "all that we are not," the struggle for socialism can bring about the Great Reversal when "we who have been naught, shall be all."

The basic antagonisms in economics and politics distort the relations of people in all other domains of life under capitalism from their emotional responses to one another up to their most general ideas. This has been felt and expressed in much of the art and literature of the bourgeois epoch. The estrangement of the creative artist from the bourgeois environment, which buffets him between crass commercialism and cruel indifference, has been a perennial scandal. The cries of protest in the works of such contemporary writers as Henry Miller and Norman Mailer testify that this remains a running sore.

Something new has been added to this schism between the intellectuals and the ruling class in our own day. This is the breach that suddenly opened up between the scientists and the monopolists with the advent of the atomic bomb.

Capitalist society in its progressive period was the foster father of modern natural science and for several centuries the two pulled forward together. Most scientists in the English-speaking world took the preestablished harmony of the two so much for granted that they went about their work without concern over its social applications and ultimate consequences. The chain reaction issuing from the release of nuclear energy blasted them out of this blind comfort.

From 1942 on, nuclear physicists have found themselves in the most excruciating dilemma. They were dedicated to the discovery and dissemination of the truth for the good of all mankind. Yet the militarists turned their labor and its results against everything which they, as scientists and scholars, most cherished. "Freedom of

science" became a mockery when the results of their
research were made top secret and atomic scientists were
forcibly isolated "for reasons of state" from their fellows.

The scientists became vassalized to a military machine
serving predatory imperialist purposes, just as the industrial workers form part of the profit-making apparatus.
Instead of helping to create a better life, their achievements
dealt quicker death. Their greater command over matter
and energy was cancelled by a total lack of control over
its social uses.

What could be more inhuman than for the scientist to
become the unwilling agent of the destruction of his own
kind and the poisoner of the unborn? No wonder the
most sensitive and social-minded have cried out against
this violation of their vocation, this impermissible injury
to their inner selves. Some have refused as "conscientious
objectors" to participate in war-work; others suffered
nervous breakdowns; a few even committed suicide.

Those clustered around *The Bulletin of the Atomic Scientists* have been searching—without success—for an effective political solution. Some speak of "their collective guilt,"
although they are the victims and not the guilty ones.
The responsibility for their intolerable predicament rests
entirely upon the ruling imperialists who have thrust them
into this alienated condition.

This diagnosis indicates the only way in which they
can overcome that alienation. That is to join with those
social forces which are opposed to the imperialists and
obliged to fight them.

While the physical health of the populations in the Western World has been improving, their mental and emotional
condition has been deteriorating. This is the thesis of the
recent book *The Sane Society* in which Erich Fromm
undertakes a study of the psychopathology of modern
life. His work is particularly pertinent because the Socialist
Humanism he advocates is a psychological counterpart
of the more literary type of Humanism found in *Dissent*
and *The New Reasoner*. Fromm correctly takes issue
with those analysts who proceed from the premise that
capitalism is rational and the task of the individual is to
"adjust," that is, to conform to its special requirements.

On the contrary, he asserts, the system is inherently irrational, as its effects demonstrate. If people are to live
productively and at peace with themselves and one another,
capitalism has to go.

Fromm borrows the concept of alienation from Marx's
early writings as the central tool in his analysis of what
is wrong with the sterile and standardized acquisitive
society of the twentieth century and the main characteristics
it produces in people. He makes many astute observations
on the ways in which capitalism mangles human personalities.

He professes to criticize capitalism from a socialist stand-
point and as an admirer of Marx. But he turns Marx
upside down by declaring that Marx had a concept of
man "which was essentially a religious and moral one."
And Fromm himself tries to replace materialism with
moralizing as the theoretical basis for socialism.

This former psychoanalyst denies that the basic cause
of the sickness of modern society is rooted in the relations
of production, as Marxism teaches. They are just as much
due to spiritual and psychological causes, he writes. Socialism has to be infused with the wisdom of the great religious
leaders who taught that the inner nature of man has to
be transformed as much as his external circumstances.
He agrees with the Gospels that "the kingdom of Heaven
is within you." "Socialism, and especially Marxism, has
stressed the necessity of the inner changes in human beings, without which economic change can never lead to
the 'good society.'"

Nothing less will do the job than "simultaneous changes
in the spheres of industrial and political organization, of
spiritual and psychological orientation, of character structure and of cultural activities." His practical program for
curing the ills of modern society rejects the conquest of
power by the workers and the nationalization of industry
and planned economy. That is the way to totalitarian
regimentation, in his opinion.

He proposes the establishment of small agricultural
and industrial "Communities of Work" as hothouses in
which the laboratory conditions will be created for the
cultivation of the good life. Capitalist society is to be re-

constructed and humanity regenerated through utopian colonies like those advocated by Owen, Fourier, Proudhon and Kropotkin, which were tried and found wanting over a century ago in the United States.

Thus the "Communitarian Socialism" of this Humanist turns out to be a faded copy of the utopian fantasies of the last century. It is a form of flight from the real facts of modern technology which demand large-scale production on a universal scale to sustain and elevate the expanding population of the globe. It is also an evasion of the pressing tasks involved in eliminating the evils of capitalist reaction and Stalinism, because it alienates itself in theory and practice from revolutionary Marxism. This is the only social movement, class power and political program that can effectively abolish the rule of monopoly capitalism, uproot Stalinism, and create the material setting for a free and equal social system.

Are the alienations from which man suffers incurable? This is the contention of the Catholic Church, pessimistic Protestant theologians like Reinhold Niebuhr, existentialist followers of Kierkegaard, and some interpreters of Freud. They picture man as eternally torn and tormented by irreconcilable aims and impulses, doomed to despair and disappointment in the unending war between his deepest spiritual aspirations and his insuperable limitations as an earthbound mortal.

The historical materialists squarely oppose all such preachers of original sin. Mankind does not have eternal insurmountable failings which have to be compensated for by the fictitious consolations of the church, the mystical intuitions of idealist philosophers, or the infinitely repeated but ever defeated efforts at self-transcendence of the existentialists. The real alienations which cripple and warp humanity have ascertainable historical roots and material causes. Far from being eternal, they have, as has been indicated, already shifted their axis in the course of social development from the contest between society and nature to the conflicts within the social structure.

These internal social antagonisms are not everlasting. They do not spring from any intrinsic and inescapable evil in the nature of mankind as a species. They were generated by specific historico-social conditions which have been uncovered and can be explained.

Now that humanity has acquired superiority over nature through triumphs of technology and science, the next great step is to gain collective control over the blind forces of society. There is only one conscious agency in present-day life strong enough and strategically placed to shoulder and carry through this imperative task, says Marxism. That is the force of alienated labor incorporated in the industrial working class.

The material means for liberating mankind can be brought into existence only through the world socialist revolution which will concentrate political and economic power in the hands of the working people. Planned economy of a socialist type on an international scale will not only enable humanity to regain mastery over the means of life; it will immeasurably enhance that collective control. The reconstruction of social relations will complete the mastery of nature for social purposes initiated under class society, and thereby abolish the conditions which in the past permitted, and even necessitated, the subjugation of man to man, the rule of the many by the few.

Once everyone's primary needs are capable of satisfaction, abundance reigns, and the labor time required to produce the necessities of life is reduced to the minimum, then the stage will be set for the abolition of all forms of alienation and for the rounded development of all persons, not at the expense of one another, but in fraternal relation.

The abolition of private property must be followed by the wiping out of national barriers. The resultant increase in the productive capacities of society will prepare the way for the elimination of the traditional antagonisms between physical and intellectual workers, between the inhabitants of the city and the country, between the advanced and the undeveloped nations.

These are the indispensable prerequisites for building a harmonious, integrated, inwardly stable and constantly developing system of social relations. When all compulsory inequalities in social status, in conditions of life and labor, and in access to the means of self-development are done away with, then the manifestations of these material inequalities in the alienation of one section of society from another will wither away. This in turn will foster the conditions for the formation of harmonious individuals no longer at war with each other — or within themselves.

Such are the radiant prospects held out by the socialist revolution and its reorganization of society as projected by the masters of Marxism.

This, too, was the goal toward which the Soviet Union, the product of the first successful workers revolution, was heading under the Stalinist regime, honest Communists believed. Had they not been assured by Stalin that socialism had already been realized in the Soviet Union and it was on the way to the higher stage of communism?

Khrushchev parroted these claims. But his own disclosures at the Twentieth Congress and the outbursts of opposition in the Soviet zone since then have ripped through the delusion that a socialist society has already been consummated there. The false ideological structure fabricated by the Communist Party machine lies shattered. How are the pieces to be put together again, and in what pattern?

The first thing that has to be done is to go back and check what actually exists in the Soviet Union at its present point of development with the fundamentals of Marxist theory. In their own way some of the "humane" socialists try to do this. "It was assumed," Thompson, editor of *The New Reasoner,* writes, "that all forms of human oppression were rooted, ultimately, in the economic oppression arising from the private ownership of the means of production; and that once these were socialized, the ending of the other oppressions would *rapidly* ensue." (My italics.)

This proposition of historical materialism retains its full validity, even though the Humanist critics question it. What, then, went wrong? Taken by itself, this historical generalization is an abstract standard which has to be wedded to existing facts and their state of development in order to become concrete and fruitful. *The essence of the matter lies in the verbal modifier "rapidly."* Between the ending of capitalist private ownership and the elevation of the nationalized means of production to the level of socialist abundance there has to be a transition period in which features carried over from the old bourgeois order are intermingled with the fundamental institutions of the new society in the making.

In the case of the Soviet Union this intermediate period was neither so short nor so favorable in its setting as the forecasts of Marx and Lenin anticipated. This historical stage has stretched out over four agonizingly difficult decades and is still far from concluded. The obligation of a scientific socialist is to study the real conditions of the economic and social development of the first workers state over these forty years in the light of all the guiding generalizations of his method. He must inquire to what extent the material circumstances have approached the theoretical norm; wherein they fell short and why; and then determine the ways and means required to bridge the gap between the existing state of affairs and the ideal standard.

Thompson and his fellow Humanists, however, dismayed by the ugly features of Stalinism suddenly bared to their vision, proceed quite differently. They carelessly toss out the historical generalizations, which condense within themselves an immense wealth of experience and analysis of social development, along with their disfigured expressions in real life. This is not the first time that well-intentioned radicals, thrown off balance by the contradiction between the standards of what a workers state should be and its political degeneration under the Stalinist regime, have rejected both the theoretical norm and the existing reality. After having been cradled so long in illusions, they cannot face the objective historical facts of the Soviet structure.

Marxist sociology, however, demands that the facts as they are be taken as the starting point for theory and action. What are these facts?

In June 1957 Khrushchev swore over TV that there are no contradictions in Soviet society. This was no more credible than his assertion that all was well with the new "collective leadership"—shortly before Molotov, Malenkov, Kaganovitch and other dignitaries were cashiered. The more prudent Mao Tse-tung admitted that certain types of contradiction can exist between the government and the people in the workers states but that those in China, and by inference the Soviet Union, are exclusively of the non-antagonistic, non-violent kind.

The divergences between the bureaucrats and the masses in the Soviet Union which have produced the all-powerful states give the lie to these theoretical pretensions of the leaders in Moscow and Peking. How is this estrangement between the rulers and the ruled to be explained?

The taking of power by the workers and public ownership of the means of production, especially in backward countries, cannot in and of itself and all at once usher in socialism. These achievements simply lay down the political and legal conditions for the construction of the new society. In order to arrive at socialism, the productive forces have to be promoted to the point where consumer goods are cheaper and more plentiful than under the most beneficent capitalism.

This cannot be attained within the confines of a single country, as the orthodox Stalinists claim, or by adding up separated national units, each following "its own road to socialism," as the dissident Stalinists maintain. The poverty in consumer goods arising from the inferior productivity of the economy divorced from world resources is the material source for the growth and maintenance of malignant bureaucratic tumors within the most "liberal" of the workers states.

In principle, in essence, the prime causes of the alienation of labor *under capitalism*—private property in the means of production and the anarchy of the profit system—have been eradicated in the Soviet countries. Thanks to nationalization of basic industry, control of foreign trade and planned economy, the working people there are no longer separated from the material means of production but are reunited with them in a new and higher form.

However, these anti-capitalist measures and methods do not dispose of the problems of Soviet economy. Far from it. To uproot the social alienations inherited from the barbarous past, the workers states require not only a powerful heavy industry but also a well-proportioned economy that can provide the necessities and comforts of life in increasing volume to all sections of the people.

Not one of the existing post-capitalist states has raised its economy anywhere near that point. These states have not yet even approached the productivity in the sphere of subsistence and the means of culture attained by the most advanced capitalist countries. The prevailing scarcities have resulted in tense struggles among the various sectors of their population over the division of the restricted national income. In these struggles the bureaucratic caste which has cornered all the instruments of political power plays the commanding role. The rulers decide who gets what and how much. They never forget to place themselves at the head of the table.

There is no exploitation of labor as in capitalist society. But there are sharp distinctions between the haves, who make up a small minority, and the have-nots, the majority of the working population. The manifest inequalities in the distribution of available goods and amenities erode the ties of solidarity between various parts of the population and dig deep-going differences in their living standards, even where these are somewhat improved. In this sense, the product of their labor still escapes the control of the producers themselves. When it enters the domain of distribution, their production passes under the control of the uncontrolled bureaucracy. In this way their own production, concentrated in the hands of omnipotent administrators, once again confronts the masses as an alien and opposing force.

Herein is the principal source, the material basis, of the alienation of rulers and ruled in the degenerated and deformed workers states of the Soviet zone. Their antagonisms express the growth of two opposing tendencies in the economic structure: one carried over from the bourgeois past, the other preparing the socialist future. The socialist foundations of nationalized industry and planned economy in the field of production are yoked to bureaucratically administered bourgeois standards which determine the maldistribution of the inadequate supplies of consumer goods.

The development of these two contradictory tendencies

is responsible for the friction which threatens to flare up into explosive conflicts.

Why don't the workers have control over the distribution of their product? Because they have either lost direct democratic control over the state apparatus, as in the Soviet Union, or have yet to acquire it, as in the Eastern European satellites and China. Just as the workers should enjoy higher living standards under socialism than under capitalism, so in a normal workers state they should participate far more fully in the administration of public functions, enjoy more freedom and have more rights than under the most democratic of the bourgeois regimes.

There was a foretaste, and a solemn pledge, that such would be the case in the seething democracy that characterized the first years of the Soviet Republic. The subsequent political victory of the bureaucratic upstarts reduced to zero the democratic functioning of the Communist Party, the trade unions, the Soviets, the youth and cultural organizations, the army and other institutions. The powers and rights supposedly guaranteed to the people by the Soviet Constitution were in practice nullified by the centralized caste governing through Stalin's one-man dictatorship.

This autocratic system of political repression fortified the economic suppression. Through the spy system and the secret police, the jails and concentration camps, the penal powers of the state were directed far less against the forces of the overturned order than against the workers who were the bearers of the new order.

Instead of being an agency for carrying out the decisions of the people, the ultra-bureaucratized state confronted the workers and peasants, the intellectuals and youth, as well as the subject nationalities, as a parasitic, oppressive and hostile force which they yearn to throw off their backs.

Lenin envisaged, and the program of the Bolsheviks stated, that the workers would control and manage industry through their elected representatives. Instead, the division of economic functions which excludes the workers under capitalism from exercising their initiative, intelligence and will has been recreated in new forms under the bureaucratic maladministration of the Soviet economy.

"The universal brain" which supervises production is no longer the capitalists—but it is also not yet the workers as it should be under a genuine Soviet democracy. The hierarchy of bureaucrats arrogated all major powers of decision to themselves under the successive five-year plans. Orders were issued from the single centralized command post in Moscow, even on matters of detail. All science and judgment were vested in appointed officials. Decentralization of industrial management since Stalin's death has modified but not essentially changed this setup.

The workers neither propose nor dispose freely of their energies in the labor process. They do not initiate the plan, participate in its formulation, decide its allotments, apply, oversee, and check up on its operation and results. They are relegated to the role of passive objects, subjected to unremitting exhortations and harsh forms of pressure to perform their tasks better.

The workers on the job are speeded up by means of piece-work and arbitrary setting of work norms. Until the reforms of the late-1950s they were chained to their jobs in the factories by workbooks and internal passports and liable to severe penalties for infractions of the rules and for being minutes late to work. They have no right to strike against intolerable conditions.

Meanwhile they see the multiplication of parasites in directing positions and gross mismanagement of the nation's resources. Reports by Soviet officials themselves have cited many instances of such industrial waste and disorganization.

Thus the plan of production, which should be collectively adopted and carried through by the producing masses, appears as an alien pattern imposed upon them by heartless functionaries in disregard of their wishes and welfare.

The Soviet bureaucracy is itself the living embodiment of a gigantic fraud. This privileged, anti-socialist force is obliged to parade as the representative and continuator of the greatest movement for equality and justice in history while riding roughshod over the most elementary needs and feelings of the working people. This immense disparity between its progressive pretentions and its reactionary course is at the bottom of the hypocrisy and deceit that mark Stalinized regimes.

Their "dictatorship of the lie" permeated every department of Soviet life. From the top to the lower depths the Soviet people were forced to lead double lives: one for public show conforming to the official line of the moment; the other, of suppressed resentment and frustration at their inability to express their real thoughts and emotions lest they be handed over to the Inquisition.

They became alienated from the regime which alienated them from their deepest thoughts and feelings and from one another. "The worst in our system was not the poverty, the lack of the most essential necessities, but the fact that this system made life one great big lie, having to listen to lies, to read lies every hour of the day, all day long, and being forced to lie oneself in turn," a nameless Budapest intellectual complained to a German reporter.

The revulsion against such spiritual degradation was one of the main causes behind the uprising of Hungarian and Polish intellectuals and youth. It is also one of the main themes of the newly awakened, critical-minded generation of Soviet writers. They are articulating as best they can the rankling protest against regimentation of cultural, scientific and artistic activities; against the suffocating atmosphere of double-talking and double-dealing; against official impostures that not only stifle creative work but make even normalized existence difficult.

In the "People's Democracies" of Eastern Europe, in the Baltic countries, the Ukraine and other oppressed nations within the Soviet Union itself there is another source of resentment: the grievance against a Great Russian regime which governs heedless of the special demands, traditions, autonomy and interests of the oppressed nationality.

Religion is primarily the product of mankind's lack of control over the forces of nature and society. The socialist movement has as one of its objectives the abolition of the material conditions which permit such degrading fictions to stunt people's outlooks and cramp their lives.

The influence of orthodox religion has been considerably curtailed by atheist education in the Soviet Union since the Revolution. But in its stead there arose that secular "cult of the individual," the deification of Stalin. This revival of idolatry is all the more startling and paradoxical because it emerged, not from the most unenlightened strata of the population, but on the very heights of the ruling Communist Party which was avowedly guided by the materialist philosophy of Marxism. The working class anthem, the *Internationale*, says: "We need no god-given saviors." Yet the Soviet peoples and the Communist parties were indoctrinated with the myth of the infallibility of the all-wise "savior" in the Kremlin.

How did the practices of the Roman and Byzantine empires, which deified their emperors, become duplicated in the first workers state?

The answer is not to be found in the exceptional virtues or vices of Stalin but rather in the role he performed for the privileged bureaucratic caste. Having elevated itself as the sole ruling power, it could no more practice democracy within its own circle than it could permit democracy in the country as a whole. It was necessary to find other means of solving the internal problems and conflicts. The means had to be in consonance with the methods of rule: autocratic, violent and deceitful.

Stalin took supreme command, and held it unchallenged for so long, because he best fulfilled the assigned function of the ruthless, all-powerful, omniscient arbiter. Just as the bureaucracy settled everything in the country, "the man of steel" decided everything within the bureaucracy and for it.

The power of the gods, indeed, their very existence, was at bottom derived from the powerlessness of the people in the face of society and nature. So the almighty power of the idolized Stalin was based upon the total usurpation of power from the people. The cult of the individual, so persistently inculcated for decades, was its end-product. The raising of Stalin to superhuman heights was the other side of the political degradation of the Soviet workers.

The breakup of the cult of the individual has been brought about by the reverse process: the growing strength of the Soviet working class and the weakening of the positions of the bureaucracy as a result of the postwar developments. Stalin's heirs are trying — without much success — to substitute the more impersonal cult of the bureaucracy under the title of "the collective leadership" for the downgraded cult of the individual.

When the people get off their knees, the high and mighty rulers no longer loom so large. As the workers regain their self-confidence and feel their collective strength, their former prostration before fabricated idols vanishes. The outraged revolutionists of Budapest who pulled down the statue of Stalin on the first day of their uprising showed by that symbolic act the fate in store for all the bureaucratic overlords.

The experience of the post-capitalist regimes over the past forty years has shown that the danger of bureaucratic distortion and degeneration of the workers states in the transitional period from capitalism to socialism is genuine.

This danger does not flow from any innate evil in a human nature which has an unslakable thirst for power, as the moralizers insist. It arises from the surrounding material conditions, from the inadequacy of the powers of production to satisfy the wants of the people, even under the most progressive social forms. This economic situation enables the specialists in administration to mount once more upon the backs of the masses and erect their regime, for a time, into an instrument of oppression. The more impoverished and undeveloped the country is, the more menacing this danger becomes. While overproduction is the curse of capitalist economy, underproduction is the curse of the socialized economies.

The causes and character of the malady which has infected the first workers states indicate the measures that must be taken to counteract it, so far as that is possible under the given circumstances. *The prescription for the cure is nothing less than democratic control of both the government and the economy by the masses of working people.*

The real power must be exercised through councils freely elected by the manual and intellectual workers of city and country. Their democratic rights should include freedom of organization and propaganda by all parties which recognize and abide by the gains of the revolution; freedom of the press; all public functionaries to be under the control of the electorate with the right of recall of representatives on all levels.

There must be such political reforms as the restoration of democracy within the workers' parties with control of the leadership and policies by their members; the restriction of the income of officials to that of the most skilled workers; the drawing of the people into the administration of public functions; the abolition of the secret police, internal passports, labor camps for political dissenters and other abominations.

In the economic domain the workers must have control over national planning and its execution on all levels and at all stages so that timely reviews can be made of results in the light of actual experience. Wage standards and other means of distribution must be revised so that inequalities can be reduced to the minimum. The trade unions should have the right to strike in order to safeguard the workers against mistakes and abuses of their government.

All nationalities should have the right to be independent or to federate, if desired, in a fraternal and equal association of states.

Such measures would add up to a revolutionary change in the structure and operation of the existing workers' states, a salutary change from bureaucratic autocracy to workers' democracy.

How is such a transformation to be accomplished? Not by concessions doled out from above by "enlightened absolutism" or a frightened officialdom but through direct action by the working people themselves. They will have to take by revolutionary means the rights of rulership which belong to them, which were promised by the Marxist program, and which were denied them by the bureaucratic usurpers.

The "humane" socialists bracket Stalinism with capitalism because both, they say, subjugate men to things and sacrifice the creative capacities of mankind to the Moloch of "economic necessity." Let us agree that, despite their opposing economic foundations, the Stalinist regimes do exhibit many similarities with the states of the capitalist world. But these points of identity do not arise from their common exaltation of things above men. They have a different origin.

Under the guise of defending the free personality against the coercion of things, the neo-Humanists are really rebelling against the facts of life formulated in the theory of historical materialism. All societies have been subject to severe economic constraint and must remain so up to the advent of future communism. The less productive a society is and the poorer in the means of subsistence and culture, the harsher these forms of constraint must be. The mass of mankind must labor under this lash until they raise the powers of production to the point where everyone's needs can be taken care of in a work week of ten hours or less.

This reduction of necessary labor will free people from the traditional social load that has weighed them down and enable them to devote most of their time to general social welfare activity and personal pursuits and pastimes. Recent developments in science, technology and industry from nuclear energy to automation place such a goal within sight. But our society is still quite a distance from this promised land.

The means for such freedom cannot be provided under capitalism. They have not yet been created in the transitional societies that have passed beyond capitalism. So long as the workers have to toil long hours daily to acquire the bare necessities of existence and compete with one another for them, they cannot administer the general affairs of society or properly develop their creative capacities as free human beings. Such social functions as government, the management of industry, the practice of science and the arts will continue to be vested in specialists. Taking advantage of their posts of command, these specialists have raised themselves above the masses and come to dominate them.

It is out of these economic and social conditions that the ultra-bureaucratic police regimes of the workers' states have arisen. There, as under capitalism, though in different forms, the privileged minority prospers at the expense of the labors of the majority.

The evils of Stalinism do not come from recognizing the material limitations of production or acting in accord with them. Even the healthiest workers regime would have to take these into account. The crimes of Stalinism consist in placing the interests and demands of favored functionaries before the welfare of the people and above the needs of development towards socialism; in fostering inequalities instead of consciously and consistently diminishing them; in concealing both the privileges of aristocrats and the deprivations of plebeians; in stripping the workers of their democratic rights — and trying to pass off these abominations as "socialism."

The task of eradicating the scourge of bureaucratism in the post-capitalist states is inseparable from the task of abolishing bourgeois rule in capitalist countries. The role of the Kremlin hierarchy has been no less pernicious in foreign affairs than at home. If the menace of imperialist intervention has helped the bureaucracy to maintain its power, its international policies in turn have been a prime political factor in saving capitalist rule from being overthrown by the workers.

By imposing policies of class collaboration upon the Communist parties, Stalin rescued tottering capitalist regimes in Western Europe at the end of the Second World War. At the same congress where he made his secret report on Stalin's crimes (omitting this one, among others!) Khrushchev made a declaration of policy on "new roads to socialism" which was essentially Stalin's old course rendered more explicit. He stated that Lenin's analysis of the imperialist stage of capitalism and the revolutionary struggle of the workers against it was outmoded by new world-historical conditions. According to Khruschev, not only are there no conflicts within Soviet society but even the contradictions between monopolist reaction and the workers which provoked revolutionary actions in the past have become softened. The existing capitalist regimes may now, under certain conditions, be magically transformed into People's Democracies by reformist methods and through purely parliamentary channels.

The Stalinist bureaucracy and the parties it controls do not propose to follow the path of leading the revolutionary activities of the masses to the conquest of power. They rather seek a general agreement with Western capitalists to freeze the present map of the world and its relationship of class forces.

This reciprocal reliance of capitalist rulership upon Stalinist opportunism, and Stalinist opportunism upon "peace loving" capitalists, whereby one sustains the other at the expense of the world working class, can be broken up only by an international movement of the masses which is both consistently anti-imperialist and anti-Stalinist.

The question of alienation ultimately merges with the long-standing problem of the relation between human freedom and social necessity. Socialism promised freedom, cry the new Humanists, but see what terrible despotism it has begotten under Stalinism. "Are men doomed to become the slaves of the times in which they live, even when, after irrepressible and tireless effort, they have climbed so high as to become the masters of the time?" asks the imprisoned ex-Communist leader and newly converted Social Democrat Milovan Djilas in the autobiography of his youth, *Land Without Justice.*

How does historical materialism answer this question? The extent of man's freedom in the past was rigidly circumscribed by the degree of effective control society exercised over the material conditions of life. The savage who had to spend most of his waking hours every day of the year chasing after food had little freedom to do anything else. This same restriction upon the scope of human action and cultural development has persisted through civilization for the bulk of mankind — and for the same economic reasons.

If people suffer today from the tyranny of money or from the tyranny of the state, it is because their productive systems, regardless of its property forms, cannot at their present state of development take care of all their physical and cultural needs. In order to throw off these forms of social coercion, it is necessary to raise the powers of social production — and, in order to raise these powers, it is necessary to get rid of the reactionary social forces which hold them back.

Scientific socialists can agree with the new Humanists that it is necessary to live up to the highest moral standards. They recognize that the desires for justice, tolerance, equality and self-respect have become as much a part of civilized life as the needs for food, clothing and shelter. Marxism would not be fit to serve as the philosophical guide of the most enlightened people of our time if it failed to take these demands into account.

But that is only one side of the problem. Until their basic material requirements are actually assured for everyone, the higher activities are stunted and social relations must remain un-humanized. The forces of reaction, whose codes and conduct are governed by the will to defend their power, property and privileges at any price, determine the moral climate far more than their opponents who have more elevated aims and ideals.

It would be more "humane" for the Western imperialists to withdraw quietly from their colonial domains, instead of fighting to hold them. But the actions of the French in Algeria again prove that ruthless terror, not peaceful reason, is more likely to prevail.

From the economic, cultural and ethical standpoints, it would be preferable if the monied magnates would recognize that their usefulness is finished and consent to yield their possessions and power to the socialist workers movement by mutual agreement between the contending classes. So far history has not provided any such sensible and straight-forward solution to the transition from capitalism to socialism.

The principal task before the Soviet people is to get rid of the archaic monstrosity of their totalitarian political structure. It would be best if the Stalinist leaders would give up their functions as an oppressive ruling caste, grant independence to their satellites, and return complete power to their own people. But the cases of Hungary and Czechoslovakia indicate that they are unlikely to cede their commanding positions gracefully, gradually or easily.

"Humane" and "reasonable" solutions to the fundamental social problems of our time are blocked by these bulwarks of reaction. That is why the anti-capitalist revolutions in the advanced countries, the anti-imperialist movements in the colonies, and the anti-bureaucratic struggles in the

Soviet zone will have to be brought to successful conclusions before the causes of the antagonisms which plague
mankind can be eliminated.

Over a century ago Marx emphasized that people cannot
behave according to truly human standards until they
live under truly human conditions. Only when the material
conditions of their existence are radically transformed,
when all their time becomes available for freely chosen
pursuits, can they throw off the contradictory relations
which have tormented mankind with separatism and conflict.

The aim of socialism is to introduce the rule of reason
into all human activities. The alienations from which
people suffer have been produced and perpetuated by
the unconscious operation of uncontrollable natural and
social forces. Socialism will eradicate the sources of alienation by bringing under conscious control all those hitherto
unmanageable forces which have crippled mankind, frus-
trated its deepest aspirations, and thwarted its full and
free development in any desired direction.

This process will start by eliminating the irrationality,
anarchy and inadequacy of the economic foundations
through planned production of the necessities of life and
the means of cultural development. In this age of nuclear
energy, electronics and automation the linking up of the
workers' republics in the industrialized countries with those
in less developed lands, can, within a measurable period,
bring the productive powers of society to the point where
there can be abundance for all, for the economically re-
tarded as well as for the most advanced peoples.

As this economic goal is approached, the conditions
will be prepared for the reduction of all governmental
compulsions over the associations and actions of people,
culminating in the abolition of man's power over man.
The universal elevation of living and educational standards will break down the opposition between workers and
intellectuals so that all intelligence can be put to work
and all work be performed with the utmost intelligence.
In this new form of social production labor can become
a joyous and significant enterprise instead of an ordeal.

The progress of science will be planned to create the

most worthy conditions for the all-sided improvement of humanity. The supreme aim of socialism is humanistic in the highest and deepest sense. It is nothing less than the remaking of the human race in a thoroughly conscious and scientifically planned manner.

The scientists of socialism will not only penetrate into galactic space. They will invade the remotest hiding places of matter, and especially living matter. They will systematically seek out and subdue the obscure forces at work in their own bodies and psyches, the legacy of blind animal evolution.

With knowledge and power thus acquired, humanity will become the freely creative species it has the potential of becoming. Men will re-create their natural environment, their organisms and their mutual relations as they wish them to be. To human beings of that happier time the welfare of their fellows will be the first law of their own existence.

All economy is economy of labor time and freedom comes down in the last analysis to freedom from compulsory labor. The expenditure of time and energy in procuring the material means of existence is an inheritance from the animal state which prevents people from leading a completely human life. Humanity will suffer from this alienation so long as it must engage in socially necessary labor.

The Bible says: "In the sweat of thy face shalt thou eat bread." This has been the lot of humanity throughout the ages. The members of primitive communities are the slaves of labor time as well as the members of class society. Savages, however, work only for themselves and not to enrich others.

The laboring force in class society has to produce extra wealth for the owners of the means of production in addition to their own upkeep. They are doubly enslaved by surplus labor time piled upon necessary labor time. The wage workers who are obliged to create an ever-expanding surplus of value for the masters of capital are more intensively sweated than any other class.

It is not the socialist but the capitalist who looks upon labor as the essence of humanity and its eternal fate.

use in the conclusion OK

Under capitalism the wage worker is treated, not as a fellow human being, but as a mechanism useful for the production of surplus value. He is a prisoner with a lifetime sentence to hard labor.

Marxism assigns the highest importance to labor activity, recognizing that production of wealth beyond the mere means of subsistence has been the material basis for all advancement in civilization. But Marxism does not make an idol of labor. For all its mighty accomplishments, to work for a living is not the height of human evolution or the ultimate career of humanity. Quite the contrary. Compulsory labor is the mark of social poverty and oppression. *Free time for all is the characteristic of a truly human existence.*

Put all this in!

The necessity for labor remains, and may even for a time become more imperious, after capitalist relations are abolished. Although people no longer work for exploiting classes but for a collective economy, they do not yet produce enough to escape the tyranny of labor time. Under such conditions labor time remains the measure of wealth and the regulator of its distribution.

But, contrary to the situation under capitalism, the greater their powers of production grow, the closer the workers come to the hour of their release from servitude to labor. When the production of all the material necessities of life and means of culture will be taken over by automatic methods and mechanisms, requiring the minimum of superintendence, humanity will be freed to develop its distinctively human capacities and relations to the full.

The prehistory of humanity will end and its development on a truly human basis begin, when wealth of all kinds flows as freely as water and is as abundant as air and compulsory labor is supplanted by free time. Then free time enjoyed by all will be the measure of wealth, the guarantee of equality and harmony, the source of unrestricted progress and the annihilator of alienation. This is the goal of socialism, the promise of communism.